Dear Adult Student,

Learning new things and building basic skills may be challenging for you, but they also can be very exciting. When you follow the basic guidelines for learning basic skills, you will be acquiring skills that will prepare you for life.

The skills that you will study and practice in this workbook will help you become more confident as you master them. These skills can help you with many things that you do in life, such as buying a car, shopping for groceries, applying for a job, reading maps, and recognizing signs.

You may be using this workbook on your own or as part of an adult education or training program that you are enrolled in. If this is your own copy, you may want to answer the practice questions right in the workbook or on the attached answer sheet in the back. If the workbook belongs to the classroom or program that you are enrolled in and will be used by other students, you should not write in it. Use a separate answer sheet instead.

Before you start your work, it would be helpful to find out which skills you need to work on. You may have taken a test such as TABE®—*Tests of Adult Basic Education*. These tests can be used to find out what skills you already know, and also to point out which skills need more work.

Once you have identified the skills you need to work on, go to the Table of Contents, find the section for one of the skills that you want to work on, turn to that page, and start doing the practice questions.

When you have finished the practice questions, you will find an answer key at the back of the workbook. You can use the answer key to check your work.

Best wishes for a successful and useful experience in using this workbook to get information and practice on the skills that you want to learn more about and would like to master. Congratulations on continuing your education.

Mastering the skills listed below can help you achieve your goals and improve many life skills, from reading the daily newspaper to getting a better job. Talk with your teacher about the skills that you need to work on. Find a skill section that you want to work on in the list below, turn to that section in your workbook, and start practicing.

Page

READING

Interpret Graphic Information   4

Words in Context 16

Recall Information 22

Construct Meaning 28

Evaluate/Extend Meaning 46

LANGUAGE

Usage 62

Sentence Formation 80

Paragraph Development 90

Capitalization 98

Punctuation 104

Writing Conventions 110

SPELLING

Vowel 118

Consonant 124

Structural Unit 128

The answers to the problems in each section are located in the Answer Key in the back of this workbook.

INTERPRET GRAPHIC INFORMATION

Graphic information is information displayed in drawings, photographs, maps, graphs, or charts. Graphics organize information so that readers can easily and quickly find what they need to know, without having to read every word.

Interpreting Graphic Information includes subskills, such as Maps, Forms, and Consumer Materials.

The map below shows the time zones in Australia. Study the map.

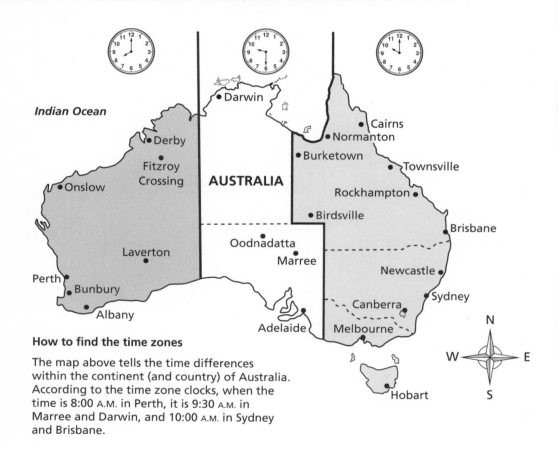

How to find the time zones

The map above tells the time differences within the continent (and country) of Australia. According to the time zone clocks, when the time is 8:00 A.M. in Perth, it is 9:30 A.M. in Marree and Darwin, and 10:00 A.M. in Sydney and Brisbane.

Look at this example.
Use the map to find the correct answer.

EXAMPLE	ANSWER
Ernie, who lives in Albany, is flying to Brisbane to visit his relatives. When he arrives, he should set his watch	• **Answer *c* is correct.** As Ernie is traveling east, he needs to set his watch *ahead*. Between Albany and Brisbane there is a time difference of *two hours.*

a   back one hour

b   back two hours

c   ahead two hours

d   ahead three hours

• **Answer *c* is correct.** As Ernie is traveling east, he needs to set his watch *ahead*. Between Albany and Brisbane there is a time difference of *two hours.*

• None of the other answer choices would show the correct time.

Time zones are regions of the Earth which have a common time.

Reminder

Use the map to answer Numbers 1 through 4.
First, try Numbers 1 and 2 for practice.

1. Emma lives in Cairns. She wants to call her sister Liza in Darwin at 11:00 P.M. Darwin time. At what time should Emma make her phone call?

   a 10:30 P.M. Cairns time

   b 11:00 P.M. Cairns time

   c 11:30 P.M. Cairns time

   d 12:00 P.M. Cairns time

   ANSWER *c* is correct. As the time in Cairns is half an hour later than it is in Darwin, Emma should make her call at 11:30 P.M. Cairns time.

2. Dimitri and his family, who live in Perth, are flying to Sydney for a vacation. Their flight leaves at 11:00 A.M. The flight will take approximately 3 hours in addition to a one-hour layover in Adelaide. Which of these is the correct arrival time for the flight Dimitri and his family are taking?

   a 2:00 P.M.

   b 3:00 P.M.

   c 4:00 P.M.

   d 5:00 P.M.

   ANSWER *d* is correct. Sydney is two hours ahead of Perth. If the total travel time is four hours, they will arrive at approximately 5:00 P.M.

Now you are ready to do more problems. The answers to the problems in this section can be found in the back of this workbook.

Now, answer Numbers 3 and 4.

3. According to the map, which of these is true?

   a When it is 7:00 A.M. in Onslow, it is 8:30 A.M. in Darwin.

   b When it is 4:00 P.M. in Perth, it is 2:00 P.M. in Rockhampton.

   c When it is 5:00 P.M. in Hobart, it is 7:00 P.M. in Derby.

   d When it is 11:30 A.M. in Marree, it is 1:00 P.M. in Burketown.

4. A map such as this is most likely to be found in

   a a dictionary

   b a thesaurus

   c an encyclopedia

   d the yellow pages

Making sense of information presented through graphics helps you read advertisements, do research, use information and reference sources, read maps, fill out forms, and perform many other daily activities.

Janine is writing a report on the history of flamenco music and dance. Using her library's computer catalog to search for sources, she receives the following results:

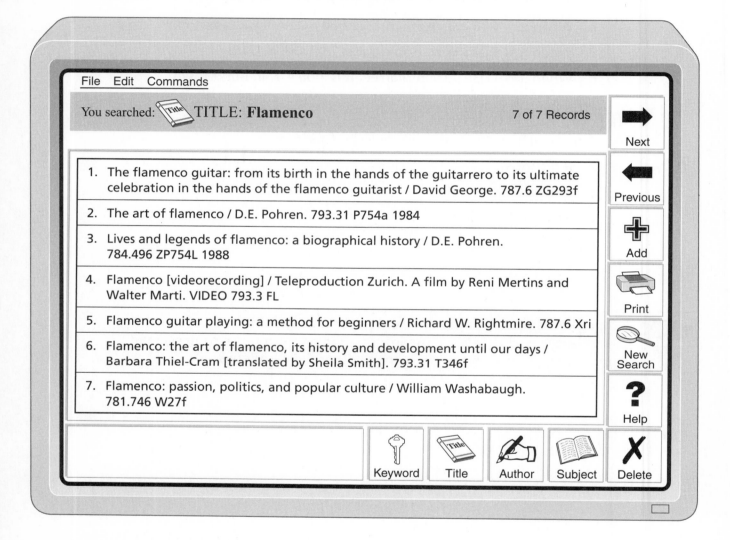

File   Edit   Commands

You searched: [Title] TITLE: **Flamenco**   7 of 7 Records

Next

1. The flamenco guitar: from its birth in the hands of the guitarrero to its ultimate celebration in the hands of the flamenco guitarist / David George. 787.6 ZG293f

2. The art of flamenco / D.E. Pohren. 793.31 P754a 1984

3. Lives and legends of flamenco: a biographical history / D.E. Pohren. 784.496 ZP754L 1988

4. Flamenco [videorecording] / Teleproduction Zurich. A film by Reni Mertins and Walter Marti. VIDEO 793.3 FL

5. Flamenco guitar playing: a method for beginners / Richard W. Rightmire. 787.6 Xri

6. Flamenco: the art of flamenco, its history and development until our days / Barbara Thiel-Cram [translated by Sheila Smith]. 793.31 T346f

7. Flamenco: passion, politics, and popular culture / William Washabaugh. 781.746 W27f

Previous

Add

Print

New Search

? Help

Keyword   Title   Author   Subject   Delete

Tip

Although titles of works should be capitalized, in a library's computer catalog you will *probably* find only the first word of a title capitalized.

Use the information in the display to answer Numbers 5 through 9.

5. Which of these would probably be *least*
   useful as a research source for Janine's report?

   a   *The art of flamenco*

   b   *Flamenco guitar playing: a method
       for beginners*

   c   *Lives and legends of flamenco:
       a biographical history*

   d   *Flamenco: the art of flamenco, its history
       and development until our days*

6. Which of these sources would probably contain
   the most information about celebrated flamenco
   musicians and dancers?

   a   *The art of flamenco*

   b   *Lives and legends of flamenco: a biographical history*

   c   *Flamenco: passion, politics, and popular culture*

   d   *Flamenco: the art of flamenco, its history and
       development until our days*

7. The *best* way for Janine to broaden her search to find
   more sources on her topic would be to search under

   a   AUTHOR: Pohren

   b   KEYWORD: history

   c   SUBJECT: flamenco

   d   TITLE WORD: guitar

Not all important information is
clearly stated. Sometimes you must use
the information given to determine
the facts you want to know.

Reminder

For Numbers 8 and 9, write your answers.

8. Which of the titles in the display is *not* a book?

   _____

9. Which of the seven records contains a title that was originally written in a language other than English?

   _____

A *biography* is a written account of a person's life; a *biographical history* is a history told through accounts of the people involved.

Answer Numbers 10 through 12 about using reference sources.

10. A map showing the boundaries of your area code would most likely be found in a

    a world atlas

    b travel guide

    c phone book

    d business directory

11. Which of these sources would probably provide the most reliable, up-to-date information about laws governing the use of copyrighted materials?

    a the website for the U.S. Copyright Office

    b the website for the Center for Business Ethics

    c a monthly magazine titled *Authors and Publishers*

    d a book titled *A History of U.S. Copyright Law*

The word *specific* means *"concerned with a **particular** subject."*

12. Which of these would be the most specific topic for a report?

    a The Olympics

    b Patricia McCormick's Winning Dive

    c The World's Olympic Gold Medalists

    d U.S. Olympic Diving Performances of the Past Twenty Years

Deni must complete the following registration form in order to enroll in a general science class at her local adult school.

REGISTRATION FORM

PLEASE PRINT   DATE: _____

NAME: _____
            (Last)   (First)   (Middle)

ADDRESS: _____
               (Street)   (Apt. #)   (City)   (State)   (Zip Code)

PHONE: (_____)_____(_____)_____ E-MAIL: _____
            (Daytime)   (Evening)

SEX: Male ☐ Female ☐

ETHNICITY (optional):

African American	Caucasian	Native American
Alaska Native	Filipino	Pacific Islander
Asian American	Hispanic	Other: _____

PRIMARY REASON FOR ENROLLMENT (circle one):

Diploma	Learn English	Job Skills
GED	Basic Skills	Personal Enrichment
Parent Education	Citizenship	Other: _____

Have you attended Bradley Adult School before? Yes ☐ No ☐ Dates: _____

Section Number	Class Title	Instructor	Meeting Time	Fee

Total Fees: _____

FORM OF PAYMENT (circle one):

Check   Money Order   Credit Card

Card Number:__ __ __ __ - __ __ __ __ - __ __ __ __ - __ __ __ __   Exp. Date:__ __/__ __

SIGNATURE: _____

NO CASH ACCEPTED.

Make checks payable to Bradley Adult School. Mail registration form and payment to Bradley Adult School, 245 S. Prentiss Blvd., Arlington, TX 76011.

Use the form to answer Numbers 13 through 16.

13. Deni is enrolling in General Science to prepare for the GED and also because she is interested in science. Which of these is the *best* way for her to complete the section of the form titled *PRIMARY REASON FOR ENROLLMENT*?

    a circle *Basic Skills*

    b circle <u>both</u> *GED* and *Personal Enrichment*

    c write "interested in science" on the line next to *Other*

    d determine which is her *main* reason and circle that option only

14. This form requires Deni to provide all of the following information *except* for her

    a date of birth

    d home address

    c course selection

    d form of payment

Read forms completely before filling them out, to get an idea of the kind of information needed and to avoid making mistakes.

15. Deni works at home. Her daytime phone number is the same as her evening number. Which of these is the *best* way for her to complete the PHONE section of the form?

PHONE (   ) _____   _____
                         (Daytime)   *(Evening)*

a   (817) 555-4632 (   ) _____

b   (817) 555-4632 (   ) same _____

c   _____ (817) 555-4632

d   (817) 555-4632 (   ) none _____

For Number 16, write your answer.

16. Which form of payment is *not* acceptable?

_____

NOTES

WORDS IN CONTEXT

The situation or background that gives meaning to a word is its *context*. For example, a "pitcher" can be either a container for holding liquids or a person who throws a baseball. The meaning of the word depends on the context in which it appears.

Words in Context includes subskills, such as Same Meaning and Opposite Meaning.

Read this paragraph about résumés.

The Résumé

The résumé—a typewritten summary of your education and work history—is often your first foot in the door when you're looking for a job. The résumé plays its most important role during the initial screening process, when the employer needs to <u>assess</u> your qualifications quickly to determine whether to grant you an interview. Résumés may be read for only 15 seconds or less during such <u>preliminary</u> screenings. This means that your résumé should be both informative and <u>concise</u>. It's a good idea to use <u>vivid</u> key words and phrases to help an employer single you out among all the other applicants. In addition, the employer should be able to <u>ascertain</u> the benefits you offer based on what you have accomplished in the past. Be as <u>explicit</u> as possible. Mention specific aspects of your past work, giving numbers if possible: "responsible for 20 children," "supervised 10 salespeople," "increased sales twenty-five percent." If your résumé is <u>effective</u>, you will need to be prepared to explain yourself at greater length at the second test: the job interview.

Look at this example.
Use the paragraph about résumés to find the correct answer.

EXAMPLE	ANSWER

Reread the sentence containing the underlined word *assess*. In that sentence, *assess* means the same as

a charge

b assign

c demand

d evaluate

• **Answer *d*** is correct. To *assess* something means to *evaluate* it.

Use the text to answer Numbers 1 through 6.
First, try Numbers 1 and 2 for practice.

1. Reread the sentence containing the underlined word *preliminary*.
   In this context, *preliminary* means about the same as

   a elaborate

   b introductory

   c contradictory

   d inconsequential

ANSWER *b* is correct. In this context, *preliminary* means *introductory*.

2. Look at the sentence containing the underlined word *concise*.
   Which of these means *the opposite of* the word *concise*?

   a wordy

   b gloomy

   c monotonous

   d presumptuous

ANSWER *a* is correct. The word *concise* means *brief*, or using a few,
well-chosen words to express an idea. *Wordy* is the opposite of *concise*.

Now you are ready to do more problems. The answers to the
problems in this section can be found in the back of this workbook.

Now use the text to do Numbers 3 and 4.

3. Look at the sentence containing the underlined word *vivid*.
   The word *vivid* means *the opposite of*

   a dull and vague

   b rude and blunt

   c uncertain and timid

   d dishonest and tricky

4. Reread the sentence containing the underlined word *ascertain*.
   To *ascertain* means

   a to utilize

   b to entrust

   c to illustrate

   d to determine

Apply

Many words have a *similar* definition and meaning. These words are called *synonyms*.

Some words have meanings that are the opposite of other words. These words are called *antonyms*.

These are examples of **synonyms:**
smart = clever

These are examples of **antonyms:**
happy ≠ sad

Use the text to answer Numbers 5 and 6.

5. Reread the sentence containing the underlined word *explicit*, as well as its neighboring sentences. In this context, *explicit* means the same as

   a precise

   b flexible

   c positive

   d courteous

6. Reread the sentence containing the underlined word *effective*. Below are four synonyms for the word *effective*. Determine which synonym best matches the way *effective* is used in the passage.

   a thriving

   b wealthy

   c successful

   d triumphant

Read the words in the shaded box below.

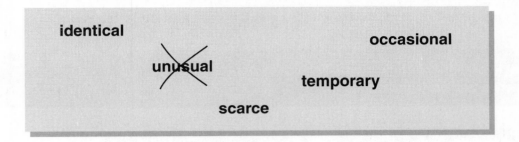

Choose the correct *antonym* from the shaded box for each of the words below. For Numbers 7 through 11, write your answers in the space provided to the right of each word. Number 7 has been done as an example.

7	ordinary	*unusual*
8	permanent	
9	abundant	
10	diverse	
11	perpetual	

RECALL INFORMATION

When you *recall information,* you remember it. Every day, you read information that you must recall. For example, you read advertisements, bills, directions for operating specialized equipment—all of these may have important information you will need to recall and use after you read it.

Recall Information includes subskills, such as Details, Sequence, and Stated Concepts.

Dylan's car battery is dead, so he asks a neighbor to help him start his car using jumper cables. The following instructions come with the cables. Read the instructions.

Attaching and Detaching Jumper Cables

— WARNING: Batteries contain corrosive acid. —

SAFETY GUIDELINES:

• Keep eyes, face, and skin away from batteries at all times and avoid touching battery with bare hands.

• Make sure vent caps are tight and level.

• Make sure the vehicles do not touch and that both engines are turned off until Step 5 directs otherwise.

1. Connect one red (positive) clamp to positive (+) post of the "dead" battery terminal.

2. Connect remaining red clamp to positive (+) post of the "good" battery.

3. Connect one black (negative) clamp to negative (−) post of "good" battery.

4. Connect remaining black clamp to engine block of stalled car, as far away from the battery as possible.

5. Start car with good battery and let idle for 15–30 seconds. Then start stalled car and immediately remove clamps, reversing procedure by removing clamp at engine block first.

Look at this example.
Use the instructions to find the correct answer.

EXAMPLE	ANSWER
According to what you read, which of these should be done *last?*	• **Answer c** is correct. Step 5 states that the jumper cables should be detached in the *reverse order* that they were attached. Therefore, since the positive clamp was supposed to be attached to the positive post of the dead battery *first,* the positive clamp should be *removed* from the positive post of the dead battery *last.*

a Remove negative clamp from the engine block of stalled car.

b Remove positive clamp from the good battery.

c Remove positive clamp from positive post of the dead battery.

d Remove negative clamp from negative post of the good battery.

• **Answers a, b,** and **d** are **not** correct. Each of those procedures should be done *before* removing the positive clamp from the positive post of the dead battery.

Use the instructions to answer Numbers 1 through 4.
First, try Numbers 1 and 2 for practice.

1. According to what you have read, during the process of attaching and detaching the jumper cables it is dangerous to

   a attach a red clamp to a positive post

   b start the car once all the cables are hooked up

   c let the engine idle for more than thirty seconds

   d come into close physical contact with the battery

   ANSWER *d* is correct. The warning at the top of the instructions states that batteries contain corrosive acid and that one should keep eyes, face, and skin away from the battery.

2. According to the instructions, which of the following should be done *first*?

   a Start car with the dead battery.

   b Start car with the good battery.

   c Remove all clamps.

   d Let engine idle.

   ANSWER *b* is correct. According to the instructions, the car with the good battery has to be started first.

Now you are ready to do more problems. The answers to the problems in this section can be found in the back of this workbook.

Complete these sentences with the correct answer.
For Numbers 3 through 5, write your answers.

3. The boldface instructions at the top are mostly concerned

   with ensuring _____.

4. A time lapse of _____ should pass after starting
   the car with the good battery and before starting the stalled car.

5. Using the jumper cable instructions, number each step from 1 to 4
   according to the sequence in which each step must be done.

⬭	Connect the jumper cables following the instructions.
⬭	Start stalled car.
⬭	Remove clamps.
⬭	Let car with good battery function for 15–30 seconds.

When you answer questions
about something you have read,
use only the information given.

Read the paragraph below from a tenant's handbook issued by the Department of Consumer Affairs.

When Can the Landlord Enter the Rental Unit?

California law states that a landlord can enter a rental unit only for the following reasons:[61]

- In an emergency.
- When the tenant has moved out or has abandoned the rental unit.
- To make necessary or agreed-upon repairs, decorations, alterations, or other improvements.
- To show the rental unit to prospective tenants, buyers, or lenders, or to provide entry to contractors or workers who are to perform work on the unit.
- If a court order permits the landlord to enter.

Except in the first two situations above (emergencies and abandonment), the landlord must give the tenant reasonable advance notice before entering the rental unit, and can enter only during normal business hours (generally, 8:00 A.M. to 5:00 P.M. on weekdays).

The law considers 24 hours' advance notice to be reasonable in most situations. The tenant can consent to shorter notice and to entry at other times. Also, the landlord can give less than 24 hours' notice when it is "impracticable" to give 24 hours' notice (for example, the landlord tries to reach the tenant 24 hours in advance, but the tenant doesn't return the call).

The landlord cannot abuse the right of access under these rules, or use this right to harass (repeatedly disturb) the tenant.

If your landlord violates these access rules, talk to the landlord about your concerns. If that is not successful in stopping the landlord's misconduct, send the landlord a formal letter asking the landlord to strictly observe the access rules stated above. If the landlord continues to violate these rules, you can talk to an attorney or a legal aid organization, or file suit in small claims court to recover damages that you have suffered due to the landlord's misconduct.

---

[61] *Civil Code Section 1954.*

Reading something for the first time gives you a general idea of the text. When you read the text a second time, you begin paying attention to details. See how many details you can recall after you read something.

Use the paragraph from the tenant's handbook to answer Numbers 6 through 9.

6. Privacy laws are designed to protect tenants from

    a the intrusions of harassing landlords

    b the annoyance of door-to-door salespeople

    c being evicted because their landlord sold
       the rental unit

    d having workers they don't know visit the
       rental property

7. Which of these describes the order in which topics are addressed in the passage?

    a history of privacy laws; recent changes in the laws;
       where to find more information

    b what tenants' rights are; what landlords' rights are;
       various procedures for handling disputes

    c common violations of privacy rights; explanations of legal
       terminology; legal procedures for responding to violations

    d conditions under which a landlord may enter a unit;
       lawful procedures for entering; what tenants should do
       if their rights are violated

For Numbers 8 and 9, write your answers.

8. The landlord must give the tenant at least _____

   notice before entering the unit.

9. A landlord may enter a rental unit without giving notice to the

   tenant *only* in _____.

CONSTRUCT MEANING

You *construct meaning* from what you read when you figure out the main point, compare facts, or draw conclusions about the people or characters described. Sometimes you need to read a story more than once to get the most information.

Construct Meaning includes subskills, such as Cause/Effect, Main Idea, and Character Aspects.

Read this article about capoeira, a martial art from Brazil.

*C*apoeira is a dynamic Brazilian martial art that combines gymnastics with dance moves and music. In its recreational form, players form a circle called a *roda,* with a group of musicians and singers at the top. Participants and onlookers sing and clap while two opponents *(capoeiristas)* use intuition and ingenuity to engage in playful, rhythmic attacks and counterattacks. Their moves carry the fluidity of dance, the vitality of acrobatics, the cunning of combat, and the pulse of the music. The musicians regulate the intensity of the capoeiristas' contest by playing more or less vigorously. Capoeira has been likened to jazz, because the spontaneous exchanges between the capoeiristas and the musicians resemble a kind of improvisational conversation.

Capoeira was originally developed by enslaved Africans of Brazil as a form of self-defense used during rebellions. The musical, acrobatic, and jocular aspects of capoeira allowed slaves to practice and develop their martial art without overseers realizing they were doing anything other than playing and joking around.

Once slaveholders discovered that capoeira was actually an instrument of revolution, its practice was forbidden by penalty of death. This did not end capoeira, however, but only forced it underground. It was not until forty years after the abolition of slavery that capoeira was made lawful to teach and practice. It flourished as a form of cultural resistance even when it was not used for reasons of self-defense. Nevertheless, it was practiced mainly in underprivileged communities, although the dominant culture disapproved of it.

Today, thanks to the tireless efforts of certain Brazilian capoeira masters *(mestres)* promoting capoeira, that stigma has all but disappeared. Capoeira is now an internationally celebrated art form, with academies all over the world. A capoeira roda is a spectacular event to see; it represents not only a heroic determination to resist oppression, but also an uncompromising assertion that life be brilliant and joyful even during times of bitter struggle.

Look at this example.
Use the article about capoeira to find the correct answer.

EXAMPLE	ANSWER
This article is *mostly* about *a* why capoeiristas must be cunning and acrobatic *b* how capoeira developed into its present-day form *c* how capoeiristas and musicians relate to one another *d* why capoeira used to be viewed as a criminal offense	• **Answer *b* is correct.** The article describes capoeira, emphasizing the recreational form that is commonly practiced today. It also provides a brief historical account of capoeira.

**Use the article to answer Numbers 1 through 6.
First, try Numbers 1 and 2 for practice.**

1. According to the article, the intensity of the struggle between the capoeiristas in the roda is determined by

   a the pace and energy set by the musicians' music

   b the level of hostility between the two opponents

   c the rate of clapping by the participants in the roda

   d the time of day during which capoeira is practiced

   ANSWER *a* is correct. The article states, "The musicians regulate the intensity of the capoeiristas' contest by *playing more or less vigorously.*" In other words, how the musicians play affects how much energy the two capoeiristas will bring to their combat.

2. According to the article, capoeira has been likened to jazz because both

   a are upbeat in terms of tempo and rhythm

   b combine music and dance in a novel way

   c have their roots in the cultural practices of African slaves

   d rely heavily on improvisational communication among players

   ANSWER *d* is correct. The article states, "The spontaneous exchanges between the capoeiristas and the musicians resemble a kind of *improvisational conversation.*"

Now you are ready to do more problems. The answers to the problems in this section can be found in the back of this workbook.

When you read something, ask yourself, "What is the most important idea?" This is the *main idea*. The main idea is not often written within the story you are reading. You have to figure out what the focus of the writing is.

Now do Numbers 3 through 6.

3. Read this sentence from the article:

   Today, thanks to the tireless efforts of certain Brazilian capoeira masters (mestres) *promoting capoeira, that stigma has all but disappeared.*

   These Brazilian *mestres* most likely promoted capoeira because they wanted to

   a practice capoeira without fear of legal punishment

   b teach people to defend themselves in dangerous times

   c inspire a sense of pride for the cultural heritage of capoeira

   d show that a serious martial art could also be practiced recreationally

For Numbers 4 through 6, write your answers.

4. In the last sentence of the article, capoeira is noted primarily

   for its _____ .

   | comic features | musical complexity | life-affirming qualities | widespread popularity |

5. Capoeira is basically a _____ .

6. Capoeiristas were able to develop their martial art because they appeared to

   be _____ and joking around.

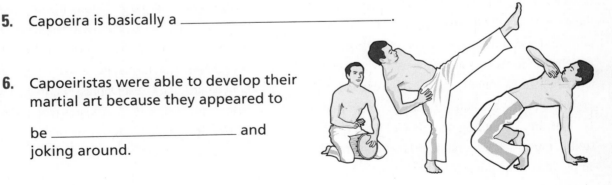

When you come to a word that you do not understand, or a word that is written in another language, use clues from the surrounding text to help you guess the meaning of the word.

Reminder

Here is a story about Jane Addams, an accomplished humanitarian whose good deeds began more than a century ago.

Jane Addams

In Chicago today, a great tree flourishes where a young woman planted a seed over a century ago. The woman was Jane Addams, and that spreading tree is Hull House. Addams was born to a well-to-do family in Cedarville, Illinois, in 1860, and was among the first generations of U.S. women to attend college. After graduation, Addams wondered how best to use her advantages in life; a trip to Europe provided an answer. She and her friend Ellen Starr visited London's Toynbee Hall settlement house, an innovative community center offering charitable services to the poor. Upon returning home, Addams convinced Starr that they should establish a similar house in an underprivileged area of Chicago.

In 1889, enlisting the help of volunteers, Addams and Starr opened Hull House. By the following year, Hull House was serving two thousand people a week, many of them immigrants. Designed to "help people help themselves," Hull House offered medical care, legal aid, childcare, and education for all ages, including enrichment in the arts and courses in vocational skills and English. Eventually, Hull House expanded to include a public kitchen, art gallery, coffee house, gymnasium, swimming pool, book bindery, art studio, music school, drama group, circulating library, employment bureau, and labor museum. Addams' and Starr's experiment succeeded beyond their wildest dreams. Across the nation, settlement houses like Hull House sprang up.

Addams spoke and wrote eloquently about settlement work, using many real-life examples to illustrate poor people's problems for her audiences. However, when economic depression hit in 1893, Addams saw that treating the effects of poverty was insufficient. Addressing its causes, she campaigned for laws to alleviate unemployment and low wages, improve working conditions and public sanitation, protect children and immigrants from exploitation, and promote equal access to education.

Throughout her life, depending on the nation's political climate, Addams sometimes drew violent criticism, especially for her efforts on behalf of labor, civil rights, and international peace. During the first World War, Addams was labeled "the most dangerous woman in America." In the 1930s, however, many of her goals became policies during the Roosevelt Administration's fight against the Great Depression. In the few years before she died in 1935, Addams received numerous honors. In 1931 she became the first American woman to be awarded the Nobel Peace Prize.

Use the story to answer Numbers 7 through 11.

7. This story is *mainly* about

   a a college graduate's quest for a fulfilling career

   b an activist's wavering reputation with the public

   c two women's efforts to start a new social movement

   d a woman's life of service to the needy and oppressed

8. In this story, Addams' settlement work is contrasted to her legislative campaigns in terms of a difference between

   a volunteering time for a cause and donating money to a cause

   b dealing with the effects of poverty and dealing with its causes

   c working for her own personal benefit and working on behalf of others

   d helping native-born Americans and helping people from other countries

Here are more questions to answer about the story.

9. In the sentence below, the author compares the results of Addams' efforts to a "great tree that flourishes":

   In Chicago today, a great tree flourishes where a young woman planted a seed over a century ago.

   Which of these details from the story best supports the author's comparison?

   a Addams was among the first generations of U.S. women to attend college.

   b Addams and Starr opened Hull House after visiting Toynbee Hall.

   c Hull House expanded to include a public kitchen, a library, and recreational and art facilities.

   d Addams became the first American woman to be awarded the Nobel Peace Prize.

Authors use *figurative language* to describe emotions, situations, or experiences in a creative way. Interpret figurative language by using your imagination. First imagine what is being described. Then ask yourself, "What else is *like* this?"

10. According to what you have read, which of these *best* describes how the 1893 economic depression affected Addams?

    a   It reduced Americans' ability to give to charities, so Addams went abroad to raise funds.

    b   It eliminated most jobs that required higher education, so Addams had to find a new goal in her life.

    c   It led the President to support the settlement movement, so Addams received more recognition for her programs.

    d   It intensified the problems of the poor, so Addams had to seek a more thorough solution than she had before.

11. During her life, Addams was first denounced as a dangerous woman, but later honored with a Nobel Peace Prize. From what you have read, which of these *best* explains such a drastic shift in how Addams was viewed by the public?

    a   The public's attitudes changed with changing times.

    b   Addams became more diplomatic in her approach to activism.

    c   Addams switched her position on certain controversial issues.

    d   The public respected older activists more than they did younger ones.

Use details from the story to help you figure out information that is not directly stated.

Tip

Here is a paragraph from Jane Addams' autobiography, *Twenty Years at Hull House.* In this paragraph, Addams remembers an incident from the settlement house's first years in existence.

We were also early impressed with the curious isolation of many of the immigrants; an Italian woman once expressed her pleasure about the red roses that she saw at one of our receptions in surprise that they had been "brought so fresh all the way from Italy." She would not believe for an instant that they had been grown in America. She said that she had lived in Chicago for six years and had never seen any roses, whereas in Italy she had seen them every summer in great profusion. During all that time, of course, the woman had lived within ten blocks of a florist's window; she had not been more than a five-cent car ride away from the public parks; but she had never dreamed of faring forth for herself, and no one had taken her. Her conception of America had been the untidy street in which she lived and had made her long struggle to adapt herself to American ways.

Use the paragraph to answer Numbers 12 through 16.

12. Read this statement from the paragraph:

We were also early impressed with the curious isolation of many of the immigrants.

Which of these *best* expresses the meaning of the above statement?

a We often admired the eagerness of many immigrants to become more educated.

b We soon wondered about the private lives of many of the immigrants.

c Many of the immigrants were determined to adapt to their new surroundings in spite of homesickness and loneliness.

d The fact that many immigrants lived remarkably separate from the rest of society made an immediate impression on us.

Reminder

A *biography* is the story of a person's life as researched and told by another person. An *autobiography* is the story of a person's life as told by *that person.*

13. The fact that the Italian woman had not seen roses
in six years is evidence of

    a her preference for Italian roses

    b her reluctance to leave her home

    c how expensive store-bought flowers were

    d how difficult it was to grow roses in Chicago

14. In this passage, Addams emphasizes the contrast between

    a the woman's dreams and her actual waking life

    b what the woman says and what she actually does

    c the woman's memories of Italy and her actual experiences in Italy

    d what the woman perceives about America and what is actually the case

For Numbers 15 and 16, write your answers.

15. According to what Addams wrote, the woman could have seen American

roses had she gone to the _____.

public parks	end of her street	downtown square	summer festival

16. Read the last sentence of the passage:

*Her conception of America had been the untidy street in which she lived
and had made her long struggle to adapt herself to American ways.*

This sentence suggests that the woman's view of America may have been

overly _____.

limited	critical	practical	optimistic

Here is an adaptation of a story written by Tao Yuanming, a Chinese nature poet who probably lived from 365 to 427 A.D.

Peach Blossom Shangri-La

Many hundreds of years ago there was a man of Wuling who made his living as a fisherman. Once while following a stream he forgot how far he had gone, and suddenly came to a grove of blossoming peach trees. It lined both banks for several hundred paces and included not a single other kind of tree. Petals of dazzling and fragrant blossoms were falling everywhere in profusion. Thinking this place highly unusual, the fisherman advanced once again, wanting to see how far it went.

The peach trees stopped at the stream's source, where the fisherman came to a mountain with a small opening through which it seemed he could see light. Leaving his boat, he entered the opening. At first it was so narrow that he could barely pass, but after advancing a short distance it suddenly opened up to reveal a broad, flat area with imposing houses, good fields, beautiful ponds, mulberry trees, bamboo, and the like. The fisherman saw paths extending among the fields in all directions, and could hear the sounds of chickens and dogs. Men and women working in the fields all wore clothing that looked like that of foreign lands. The elderly and children all seemed merry.

The people were amazed to see the fisherman, and they asked him from where he had come. He told them in detail, and then the people invited him to their home and prepared a meal. Other villagers heard about the fisherman, and they all came to ask him questions. The villagers explained, "To avoid the chaos of war during the Qin Dynasty, our ancestors brought their families and villagers to this isolated place and never left it, so we've had no contact with the outside world." They asked the fisherman what the present reign was. They were not aware of the past several hundred years of history. The fisherman told them everything he knew in great detail, and the villagers were amazed and heaved sighs. After several days there the fisherman bid farewell, at which time some villagers entreated him, "Do not tell people on the outside about us."

The fisherman exited through the opening, found his boat, and retraced his route while leaving markers to find this place again. Upon his arrival home, he told some others what had happened. They went to look for the trail markers, but got lost and never found the way.

From the following list of adjectives, choose the three that *best* describe the villagers. For Number 17, write your answers.

17.

shy	warriors	religious	contented	proud
disciplined	peaceful	playful	mischievous	friendly

_____ _____ _____

Use the story to answer Numbers 18 through 21.

18. This story is mainly about

    a a war that drove many villagers out of their native land

    b a fisherman's encounter with a secret utopian settlement

    c a secluded community's efforts to reconnect with the larger society

    d a mysterious grove of peach trees thriving in the middle of the woods

19. Which of these details about the village *best* supports the conclusion that the village is prosperous?

    a paths extending in all directions

    b imposing houses and good fields

    c clothing that looked like that of foreign lands

    d villagers that were unaware of recent history

20. Which of these aspects of the story *best* supports the idea that the story is a fantasy?

   a   No one was able to locate the village ever again.

   b   The story takes place many hundreds of years ago.

   c   The villagers invite the fisherman into their homes for a meal.

   d   The villagers had been living in seclusion for many generations.

21. Which of these *best* explains why the villagers ask the fisherman not to tell anyone about them?

   a   They are afraid they may be punished for their ancestors' escape from the war.

   b   They do not want their peaceful way of life threatened by the influences of the outside world.

   c   They do not think the fisherman will be believed if he tries to tell others what he has seen.

   d   They fear that people who come searching for the village may become permanently lost in the woods.

Read this poem about a trip to Peru, a country in South America.

Journey to the Past

My country is called Peru.
I have lived here a long time.
One day, my friend said we should travel to
The high, quiet place of the ancient people.

The train creeps up the side of the mountain.
It rattles our backs against hard wood benches.
We smell fish fried crisp, seared meat, sharp spices.
Our stomachs growl. All we have is water.

The mountains grow tall.
Their peaks are like dark pieces of broken pots
Jumbled together, pushed high, shadowed against bright blue sky.
The mountainsides are thick with grass like fur.
White stones glitter like jewels in the grass.

My friend and I cannot believe how suddenly
The storied city appears high above us, like a treasure box.

Sore and stiff, but excited, we step off the train.
We must walk a long way to the city.
Our feet tread the paths the ancients made.
We see their castles, their homes, their tables.

We sit on a wall built of ancient stones.

We talk about the olden days of fire and stone
When there were no planes, no television, no phones.

We talk about this high, quiet place:
Its beauty, its grandeur, its peace.

Use the poem to answer Numbers 22 through 27.

22. The poet mainly wants readers to

    a learn about the ancient peoples

    b understand the history of the country

    c share in the experience of the journey

    d appreciate the importance of friendship

23. "Their peaks are like dark pieces of broken pots" is another way of saying that the mountains

    a appear to be very close

    b seem to have sharp edges

    c are visible through the trees

    d reveal an approaching storm

24. This poem would most likely be found in

    a a travel guide

    b a history book

    c a daily newspaper

    d a literary magazine

25. Read this line from the poem.

The storied city appears high above us, like a treasure box.

By writing this line, the poet

a   describes how large the city is

b   compares the city to a fairy tale castle

c   suggests that the hidden, ancient city has important history

d   confirms that the city has a large amount of money

26. Because of the trip, what will the author most likely do when he returns home?

a   study the politics of the country

b   write an article about how modern cities are built

c   visit a museum that displays pottery

d   research more information about the country's history

27. Which of these conclusions about the author can be drawn from the poem?

a   The poet likes big cities.

b   The poet notices the details of the scenery.

c   The poet is not interested in ancient cultures.

d   The poet does not like to travel.

NOTES

As you read, you *evaluate* by forming opinions about what you are reading. For example, when you read a newspaper article, you weigh its value by considering its factual reliability. When you read a story, you consider metaphors and symbols to discover and understand the purpose of the story.

Evaluate/Extend Meaning includes subskills, such as Fact/Opinion, Predict Outcomes, and Author Purpose.

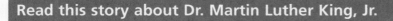

Read this story about Dr. Martin Luther King, Jr.

Dr. Martin Luther King, Jr.

Hardly a year after Martin Luther King, Jr., and his wife Coretta arrived in Montgomery, Alabama, a weary seamstress named Rosa Parks was arrested for disobeying a bus driver's order to give up her seat for a white passenger. The incident ignited the long-smoldering resentments of Montgomery's persecuted black citizens. Soon afterward, the black leaders of Montgomery formed the Montgomery Improvement Association (MIA) and asked Dr. King to lead their protest movement.

As president of the MIA, Dr. King spoke eloquently about the human dignity and the power of nonviolent resistance. He told civil rights workers, "Get the weapon of nonviolence, the breastplate of righteousness, the armor of truth, and just keep marching." Montgomery blacks sustained a 381-day boycott that nearly bankrupted Montgomery's bus line and resulted in the Supreme Court ruling against segregated buses.

As president of the Southern Christian Leadership Conference (SCLC), Dr. King devoted even more time to civil rights. In the months before 1963, Dr. King set his sights on "thoroughly segregated" Birmingham. He recruited people willing to go to jail, conducted workshops in nonviolent resistance techniques, and met with other black leaders. Thousands of black men, women, and children marched in the streets. Many demonstrators were arrested, but always there were more to take their place. People marched despite fire hoses, dogs, clubs, and armored bulldozers. Over 3,300 were jailed, including Dr. King himself.

The demonstrations made front page news all over the world and outraged millions. The sight of nonviolent protestors being met with brutality moved many people to action.

Look at this example.
Use the story to find the correct answer.

EXAMPLE	ANSWER

Which of these *best* describes what type of story this is?

a interview

b biography

c news article

d historical fiction

• **Answer *b* is correct.** A biography is a true story about someone's life. This passage tells about part of Dr. King's life.

**Use the story to answer Numbers 1 through 4.
First, try Numbers 1 and 2 for practice.**

1. Read this sentence from the story:

   The incident ignited the long-smoldering resentments of Montgomery's persecuted black citizens.

   In this sentence, the author compares the sentiments of Montgomery's black citizens to

   a a slow-burning fire

   b a high-energy laser

   c a rapidly advancing wave

   d a defiantly rebellious prisoner

   ANSWER *a* is correct. The author uses the words "ignited" and "long-smoldering" to compare the sentiments to a slow-burning fire.

2. Read this part of the story:

   Dr. King spoke eloquently about the human dignity and the power of nonviolent resistance.

   Which of these sentences from the story *best* illustrates "the power of nonviolent resistance" spoken of by Dr. King?

   a "Dr. King set his sights on 'thoroughly segregated' Birmingham."

   b "The sight of nonviolent protestors being met with brutality moved many people to action."

   c "Many demonstrators were arrested, but always there were more to take their place."

   d "The demonstrations made front page news all over the world and outraged millions."

   ANSWER *b* is correct. "The power of nonviolent resistance" came from people being moved to action by the brutality they witnessed against the nonviolent protestors.

Now you are ready to do more problems. The answers to the problems in this section can be found in the back of this workbook.

Now answer Numbers 3 and 4 about the story.

3. Choose the phrase that completes this generalization about the Rosa Parks incident most accurately: For Montgomery's black citizens, Rosa Parks' arrest

    was _____.

    a a needle in a haystack

    b a taste of their own medicine

    c the light at the end of the tunnel

    d the straw that broke the camel's back

4. Read this part of the story again:

    People marched despite fire hoses, dogs, clubs, and armored bulldozers. Over 3,300 were jailed, including Dr. King himself.

    This part of the story is probably meant to illustrate the

    a objectivity of the law enforcers

    b indifference of the general public

    c ambivalence of civil rights leaders

    d determination of the demonstrators

You *extend the meaning* of what you read by comparing it to what you already know from your own experience or from other things you have read. Sometimes you use what you know to make predictions about what might come next, or to form your own ideas.

Read the excerpt from Dr. Martin Luther King, Jr.'s famous speech, "I Have a Dream." Dr. King delivered the speech at the steps of the Lincoln Memorial in Washington, D.C., on August 28, 1963.

There is something that I must say to my people who stand on the warm threshold which leads into the palace of justice. In the process of gaining our rightful place we must not be guilty of wrongful deeds. Let us not seek to satisfy our thirst for freedom by drinking from the cup of bitterness and hatred.

We must forever conduct our struggle on the high plane of dignity and discipline. We must not allow our creative protest to degenerate into physical violence. Again and again we must rise to the majestic heights of meeting physical force with soul force. The marvelous new militancy which has engulfed the Negro community must not lead us to distrust of all white people, for many of our white brothers, as evidenced by their presence here today, have come to realize that their destiny is tied up with our destiny and their freedom is inextricably bound to our freedom. We cannot walk alone.

And as we walk, we must make the pledge that we shall march ahead. We cannot turn back. There are those who are asking the devotees of civil rights, "When will you be satisfied?" We can never be satisfied as long as our bodies, heavy with the fatigue of travel, cannot gain lodging in the motels of the highways and the hotels of the cities. We can never be satisfied as long as the Negro's basic mobility is from a smaller ghetto to a larger one. We can never be satisfied as long as a Negro in Mississippi cannot vote and a Negro in New York believes he has nothing for which to vote. No, no, we are not satisfied, and we will not be satisfied until justice rolls down like waters and righteousness like a mighty stream.

Tone refers to the overall quality, manner, or feel of a work. The language used by the author gives the work its tone.

5. Which of these *best* describes what *type* of speech this is?

    a persuasive

    b inspirational

    c informational

    d commemorative

6. Which of these *best* describes the tone of the excerpt?

    a casual

    b restless

    c solemn

    d mocking

7. Read this excerpt again:

    We will not be satisfied until justice rolls down like waters and righteousness like a mighty stream.

    Dr. King probably chose this image partly because it suggests that justice and righteousness are

    a calm and peaceful

    b beautiful but dangerous

    c common but endangered

    d powerful and unstoppable

8. In the third paragraph of the excerpt, Dr. King is *mainly* concerned with

    a laying out strategies for effective civil rights activism

    b recognizing the contributions of past civil rights activism

    c presenting the obstacles that the crusaders for the Civil Rights movement are likely to face

    d affirming devotees' dedication to the goals of the Civil Rights movement

Answer Numbers 9 through 11 about the speech.

9. Based on what you have read in this excerpt, the main purpose of Dr. King's speech was most likely

   a to inform elected officials of the intentions and aims of the Civil Rights movement

   b to teach tactics in effective nonviolent civil disobedience

   c to encourage civil rights activists to continue the pursuit of their goals through the use of nonviolent tactics

   d to persuade opponents of civil rights to sympathize with the problems and concerns of African Americans

10. In the first two paragraphs of the speech, Dr. King is *mainly* concerned with

    a the reasons why a civil rights movement is necessary

    b the means that the Civil Rights movement uses to achieve its goals

    c the resources that the Civil Rights movement has not made use of yet

    d the challenges that the Civil Rights movement will face as it grows larger

11. Dr. King uses both abstract language and concrete language in his speech. Which of these *best* illustrates the use of *concrete* language?

    a "We can never be satisfied as long as a Negro in Mississippi cannot vote. . . ."

    b "We must forever conduct our struggle on the high plane of dignity and discipline."

    c "Let us not seek to satisfy our thirst for freedom by drinking from the cup of bitterness and hatred."

    d ". . . Their destiny is tied up with our destiny and their freedom is inextricably bound to our freedom."

For Number 12, complete this chart by writing *fact* or *opinion* in the blank to the right of each sentence. The first one has been done for you as an example.

12.

Dr. King's most moving speech was the prophetic "I've Been to the Mountaintop," delivered the day before his assassination.	*Opinion*
In 1964, at age 35, Dr. King was the youngest man in history to be awarded the Nobel Peace Prize.	
Dr. King was assassinated in Memphis, Tennessee, on April 4, 1968.	
Dr. King's death was the greatest national tragedy of the twentieth century.	
It is unfortunate that few remember King for his efforts on behalf of economic justice.	

Sometimes we confuse *facts* with *opinions*. A *fact* is a statement that can be measured, observed, or proven by written records. If not, it is an *opinion*.

Reminder

Read this story about an elderly woman and a young child who has recently moved into the neighborhood.

Surprise Flowers

Mrs. Politti frowned when she saw the little boy approaching her walkway. Her new neighbors were unkempt and noisy, as neglectful of their yard as of the little boy in their care. And like the offending yard, the child had become a nuisance to others. He was always ringing her doorbell, wanting to know what she was doing, nagging her with a thousand tiresome questions. Barefoot, with dingy clothing and scabs covering his legs and arms, he was not the sort of child to make one sentimental about children. Mrs. Politti did not like to let him in. Despite her objections, however, he had clung after her like a stray mutt, loitering around her yard and waiting for her arrival, slipping unwanted tributes at her door.

"No need to keep ringing. I hear you," scolded Mrs. Politti.

"I brought you a surprise, Mrs. P.," chirped the boy as he thrust out two tightly clamped fists. "Guess."

As Mrs. Politti began to assert her indisposition for games, the boy unclenched both fists, revealing in his left a wrinkled brown paper envelope with the large penciled lettering: "SURPRISE FLOWERS." Beneath it was smaller writing she could not make out. She took the envelope. "Thank you, now you must excuse me. I have a lot of work to do," she said, and whisked him out.

In a spell of restlessness some days later, Mrs. Politti removed the wrinkled envelope from the kitchen drawer and took out her glasses.

"For An Amazing Surprise: plant 1/2 inch in the ground and water every day." She gazed out at the granite lawn, installed after her husband's death, recalling how he would toil like an elf in a wonderland, whistling amid bursting blooms and sprawling vines, as insects buzzed and flitted around him. In those days, there had been birdsong, and the tremulous dance of butterflies.

Mrs. Politti went outside and removed some pebbles from a corner of the granite lawn. The soil felt cool and pliant in her fingers. Somewhere she heard the forlorn cooing of doves. A mellow breeze lifted as she dug her fingers into the earth.

Not one to abandon a task midway, Mrs. Politti returned each morning to water the seeds. After they had pushed through the ground, she would scrutinize them vigilantly for intruding weeds and insects, until one day she was able to recognize the incognito plant. *Nasturtiums*, she thought with irony. *The child gave me seeds for growing weeds!* However, because she had come to find peace in the daily ritual of watering and checking, she continued. As the plant began to sprawl, Mrs. Politti removed more granite pebbles.

After a time, numerous tiny, tight green fists had sprung from the plant. Within days, they unclenched themselves to reveal gifts of scarlet butterfly- shaped blooms, which burst out jubilantly all over the ground, till there was hardly a spot of gray or green that could be seen.

Use the story to answer Numbers 13 through 15.

13. This story is written most like a

    a drama

    b thriller

    c comedy

    d mystery

14. The author probably believes that nasturtiums are

    a beautiful

    b annoying

    c nutritious

    d destructive

15. How will Mrs. Politti most likely be different in the future as a result of her experience with the nasturtium garden?

    a She will think less about her life with her husband.

    b She will begin to take joy in things she did not value before.

    c She will begin to develop admiration for her new neighbors.

    d She will become more relaxed about finishing what she starts.

Answer Numbers 16 through 18 about the story.

16. The author most likely uses the granite lawn to illustrate that

    a the neighborhood was experiencing a drought and had to conserve water

    b even a pile of rocks could be beautiful if arranged with care and creativity

    c Mrs. Politti had not had faith in her own ability to grow a successful garden

    d Mrs. Politti had become more practical and dispassionate since her husband's death

17. Which of these statements about the boy and the nasturtium plant probably *best* reflects the author's point of view?

    a They both are a nuisance to the neighborhood.

    b They both are unlovable through no fault of their own.

    c They both can thrive beautifully with the right care and attention.

    d They both require more patience and energy than they're worth.

18. How will Mrs. Politti probably change her behavior toward the little boy in the future?

    a She will treat him more like an adult.

    b She will try to teach him discipline and manners.

    c She will be more forceful in discouraging his visits.

    d She will be more nurturing and show him more concern.

The sound of the birds is the motif in this story. For Number 19, find the three examples of the motif. List them on the lines below.

19.

1. _____

2. _____

3. _____

A *motif* is a writing technique in which the author repeats a particular idea or theme throughout a story. The author often does this by frequently using words or phrases that relate to the idea or theme.

Reminder

Read this conversation between Maria and Charles about planning and preparing dinner.

A Special Dinner

Maria: Before we go to the supermarket we should check the list of what we need to buy. Is there anything that we should add to the list?

Charles: Oh, I almost forgot! My brother James will be here this weekend. Let's make something special for dinner Saturday night.

Maria: That's a great idea!

Charles: He is always telling me how much he loves your chicken pot pie. Do you know all the ingredients by heart?

Maria: Yes, I know all the ingredients. Okay, the first thing we'll need is a large pie crust because we won't have time to make the crust from scratch this weekend. We need to find the prepackaged ones. They are usually in the refrigerator case, near the cheese. While we are there, we need to get the cream. Let's get some ice cream for dessert, too.

Charles: Okay, pie crusts and cream. Don't forget to write that down. What else do we need?

Maria: We need a small package of chicken breasts. And which vegetables do you want? We could use any combination of peas, corn, carrots, green beans, potatoes, or broccoli.

Charles: James doesn't like peas, and you know I don't like broccoli. Let's just get corn, carrots, green beans, and potatoes.

Maria: That's fine. We'll get those in the produce section. We only need one cup of each vegetable, so we need to get a little of each—maybe a can of corn, a can of green beans, a pound or two of potatoes, and a bag of baby carrots. Then we'll need a couple of shallots.

Charles: Shallots? What's a shallot?

Maria: They're kind of like onions, but smaller—like heads of garlic, and they're red. I think they're in the produce section next to all the different onions.

Charles: *Different* onions? How many kinds of onions are there?

Maria: Well there's yellow, Vidalia, and red for starters.

Charles: OK. Do we need anything else besides shallots?

Maria: That's all we'll need for the chicken pot pie. Now we just need to decide what flavor ice cream to get. I think we should get one that is plain, like vanilla, and one that has a lot of stuff in it. What do you think?

Charles: I like any plan that means I get to buy two kinds of ice cream. How about Vanilla and Rocky Road?

Maria: Charles, we should think about what James would like to have.

Charles: He likes those flavors too. Okay, did you write it all down? Are we ready to go find everything?

Maria: We're ready. Let's go shopping!

Use this drama piece to answer Numbers 20 through 25.

20. What does Maria imply by saying "we should think about what James would like to have"?

    a They have to make the pie crust from scratch.

    b They should consider what their dinner guest likes to eat.

    c They need to decide on the ice cream flavors to buy.

    d They will need more time to make the chicken pot pie.

21. Which of these lines from the scene best states the main idea?

    a "Let's make something special for dinner Saturday night."

    b "How many kinds of onions are there?"

    c "We'll get those in the produce section."

    d "Let's just get corn, carrots, green beans, and potatoes."

22. Which of these statements is probably true of Maria?

    a She was planning to make chicken pot pie.

    b She was expecting James to visit.

    c She likes to plan and shop by herself.

    d She is an experienced cook.

23. According to the scene, what can you conclude about Maria and Charles?

    a They work well together when making plans.

    b Maria thinks James is smarter than Charles.

    c Chicken pot pie is their favorite dinner.

    d Charles knows more about cooking than Maria.

24. Which of these statements best supports the idea that Maria does more grocery shopping than Charles?

    a Maria knows the ingredients for chicken pot pie.

    b Charles chooses the flavors of ice cream they will buy.

    c Maria does not have time to make the pie crust.

    d Maria is more familiar with different types of produce.

25. Why does Charles ask Maria to make chicken pot pie for dinner?

    a Maria has always wanted to make one.

    b It is Charles' favorite dish.

    c James loves to eat it.

    d They eat it at least once a week.

NOTES

USAGE

Usage refers to the way we use words in speaking and writing. It is important that all of us use the same usage rules to help us communicate well with others.

Usage includes subskills, such as Pronouns, Verb Tense, and Subject/Verb Agreement.

Read the sentences in the following example. Find the sentence that is complete and demonstrates proper usage.

EXAMPLE	ANSWER
a The postal clerk helped us send our package.	• **Answer a** is correct. This sentence needs a pronoun in the objective case. The word *us* is the objective form of the pronoun *we*.
b I asked they to show me the way to the post office.	• **Answer b** is **not** correct. The word *they* should be replaced by the word *them*.
c She gave he a ticket with the insurance rate.	• **Answer c** is **not** correct. The word *he* is a pronoun in the nominative case, and this sentence needs a pronoun in the objective case. The correct word should be *him*.
d Ask the driver of the van if him has something for us.	• **Answer d** is **not** correct. The word *him* should be changed to the word *he*.

Look at the table below:

Nominative	Objective	Possessive
I	me	my
you	you	your
he, she, it	him, her, it	his, her, its
we	us	our
they	them	their

Look at this graphic that illustrates the use of the different cases of pronouns:

He showed **his** new car to **them.**

nominative   *possessive*   *objective*

Look at the following sentences. Choose the answer that *best* completes each sentence. First, try Numbers 1 and 2 for practice.

1. The invitation to the party was addressed to _____.

   a she and him

   b she and he

   c her and him

   d her and he

   ANSWER *c* is correct. This sentence needs a pronoun in the objective case. *Her* and *him* are both objective pronouns.

2. You should give _____ the prize for the best chili recipe.

   a he and I

   b he and me

   c him and I

   d him and me

   ANSWER *d* is correct. This sentence needs a pronoun in the objective case. *Him* and *me* are both objective pronouns.

Now you are ready to do more problems. The answers to the problems in this section can be found in the back of this workbook.

Reminder

Pronouns take three forms, or *cases*: the nominative, the objective, and the possessive.

For Numbers 3 and 4, find the sentence in each group that is complete *and* demonstrates proper usage.

3. *a* Her's car is brand new.

    b My neighbors are selling their house.

    c Are you going to Jans party Saturday night?

    d Is this filing cabinet ours' or does it belong to Susan?

4. *a* If this is you're chair, I can sit somewhere else.

    b This chair is worn, and it's legs are loose, too.

    c Do those chairs belong to Mona, or are they your's?

    d Carl's chair was squeaking, but his friend's wasn't.

Correct usage is an important part of our daily lives. For example, we should say, "*He* and *I* are playing golf today" rather than "*Him* and *me* are playing golf today." Incorrect usage often *sounds* or *looks* wrong to us. It is helpful for you to know the usage rules so you can use them correctly when speaking and writing.

For Numbers 5 and 6, find the sentence in each group that is complete *and* demonstrates proper usage.

5. *a* Both Jonathan and Laura like to cook its own dinner and help in the house.

   b Whoever has my casserole dish should return it to me immediately.

   c Every one of these dishes should go in the refrigerator, but all of it won't fit.

   d Tom and his sister couldn't hide her surprise when the winners were announced.

6. *a* "A customer is always right," said the manager, "and they should always leave the store satisfied."

   b Those cashiers are always friendly to the customers, and she will probably be promoted next month.

   c The importance of a good attitude was stressed at the last meeting, and the manager said it was the key to success.

   d Some employees are working on ways to improve customer satisfaction, so it formed a customer service committee.

The word that a pronoun refers to is called its *antecedent*. A pronoun should agree with its antecedent in both gender and number. Look at the following examples:

She gave the files to **her** boss.   The **employees** arrive at **their** stations at 5:30 A.M.

antecedent   *pronoun*   *antecedent*   *pronoun*
(feminine-singular)   *(feminine-singular)*   *(3rd person plural)*   *(3rd person plural)*

For Numbers 7 and 8, choose the word in parentheses that *best* completes each of the following sentences.

7. Every time a new version is written, newer rules and regulations make

   _____ outdated. (it / them)

8. Every day, each of the men in the station house has to do _____ share of the work. (its / his)

For Numbers 9 and 10, find the words that *best* complete each sentence.

9. If we see a movie tonight, we _____ to the theater three nights in a row.

    a had gone

    b have gone

    c had been going

    d will have gone

10. If I _____ the noise, I wouldn't have chosen this room.

    a am remembering

    b was remembering

    c had remembered

    d will have remembered

Complete each sentence with the correct form of the verb provided. For Numbers 11 through 14, write your answers.

11. Naomi went to the counseling center and _____ many career possibilities. (find)

12. Next week Brent _____ an appointment with a counselor who specializes in job placement. (make)

13. Has she ever _____ one of those vocational tests? (take)

14. We _____ the kitchen walls since noon, but we're only half finished. (paint)

Apply

The *tense* of a verb indicates when the action is occurring, such as in the past, present, or future. For example: *I **saw** you downtown yesterday. I **see** that you're here today. **Will** I **be seeing** you again soon?* Words such as *next week*, *yesterday*, and *now* will help you decide the *tense* of a verb.

Look at the example. Find the sentence that is complete *and* demonstrates proper usage.

EXAMPLE	ANSWER
a Every one of them work hard to finish the job.	• **Answer *a* is not** correct. *Every one* implies each one individually and a singular verb is required.
b The clerk has given us great help in this critical situation.	• **Answer *b*** is correct. The subject of this sentence is singular and the verb is also singular.
c What time does the employees start work?	• **Answer *c* is not** correct. *Employees* is a plural word; therefore, the question should use the word *do*.
d Are the Warehouse Department on duty today?	• **Answer *d* is not** correct. *Warehouse Department* is singular, so the verb should also be singular. The question should begin with *is*.

Now look at the following groups of sentences.
For Numbers 15 and 16, find the sentence in each group that is complete *and* demonstrates proper usage.

15. **a** Workers often transfers equipment between departments.

b Supplies and machinery are ordered by each department.

c Unauthorized equipment transfers was made by several employees.

d Even managers needs to ask for a stock transfer form.

16. **a** The cost of two new tires were more than I expected.

b An inventory of my assets is in the safety deposit box.

c Participation in the programs depend on the family's income level.

d Increases in my monthly expenses has created a financial crisis.

The subject and the verb should agree in number. If the subject is *singular*, the verb *must* be *singular*. If the subject is *plural*, the verb *must* be *plural*. For example: *The football game **is** at eight tonight. The final and semi-final tennis matches are both shown on TV.*

Reminder

Now look at Numbers 17 and 18.
Find the words that *best* complete each sentence.

17. Of all the vacation possibilities, Kim thought the desert was

    the _____.

    a   least interesting

    b   less interesting

    c   most least interesting

    d   more less interesting

18. You can buy quality equipment _____ than
    you might expect.

    a   more inexpensive

    b   most inexpensive

    c   more inexpensively

    d   most inexpensively

 Comparatives and *superlatives* may be formed using adjectives or adverbs. Use the *comparative* degree when comparing two things: *John is taller than Mary.* Use the *superlative* when comparing three or more things: *John is the tallest student in class.*

Complete each sentence with the correct comparative or superlative form of the word provided. For Numbers 19 through 23, write your answers.

19. Marina decided that the first job offer was _____ than the second one. (good)

20. I will be arriving _____ than I planned. (late)

21. He drives _____ now than before he received that ticket. (safely)

22. Of all the interviewees that day, he was the one that stayed _____ in the room. (long)

23. These roads are the _____ in town. (bad)

Look at Numbers 24 through 27. Find the sentence in each group that is complete *and* shows correct usage.

24.　*a*　The forecast wasn't very accurately today.

　　　b　The wind was very strongly and uprooted several trees.

　　　c　We could hear the rain beating constant against the windows.

　　　d　The weather hasn't been this clear in a long time.

25.　*a*　When you do this test, work as careful as you can.

　　　b　Anita felt positively about the last test results.

　　　c　I wish Sam didn't feel so bad about not getting that job.

　　　d　Which of these jobs were you thinking most serious about?

Adjectives modify or describe *nouns. Adverbs* modify or describe *verbs* and often end in *-ly*. Check to see what type of word is being modified by the word you are selecting.

26. *a* She painstakingly researches every fact in her articles.

    b This columnist writes more objective than the other one.

    c That reporter is the most respectedly journalist in the office.

    d I felt angrily when I read the editorial in yesterday's newspaper.

27. *a* The restaurant's interior is decorated very colorful.

    b This is the most unusually restaurant I've ever seen.

    c My favorite restaurant is less expensive than this one.

    d This Greek restaurant serves deliciously meals.

For Numbers 28 through 30, decide which verb to use in these sentences.

28. Ruthie _____ me how to get the lumps out of mashed potatoes. (learned / taught)

29. Animals must _____ to their environment if they want to survive. (adopt / adapt)

30. The table of contents is at the beginning of the book, so it

    _____ the letter to the student. (precedes / proceeds)

Reminder

Some verbs can cause confusion. For example, the verbs *affect* and *effect* are easily confused. *Affect* means "to impress or influence." *Effect* means "to accomplish or bring about."

Look at Numbers 31 through 33. Choose the sentence in each group that is complete _and_ demonstrates proper usage.

31. _a_ There weren't no new letters to be filed.

    _b_ The secretary temporarily didn't have nothing to do.

    _c_ He didn't leave no messages while I was at lunch.

    _d_ There was no reason to postpone going to the mailroom.

32. _a_ Sheena doesn't want no job that finishes after dark.

    _b_ Max never thought that he wouldn't find the perfect job.

    _c_ Some people don't never like jobs that involve sitting in an office all day.

    _d_ If Janine didn't want to stay inside, she shouldn't have taken no desk job.

33. _a_ The hikers had seen no sign of another person for days.

    _b_ They were sure they weren't going to be going in no straight line.

    _c_ It was so dark, he couldn't hardly tell where he was.

    _d_ Perry didn't want to take nobody else's word for it.

Avoid the use of a "double negative" such as _I **haven't never** been to the country_. Only one negative word _(no, not, none, never)_ is needed to make a sentence negative.

Reminder

The following passage about people and their pets contains some errors in usage. Read the passage and pay special attention to the underlined words.

Humans <u>have</u> animals around for companionship throughout history.
34

Nevertheless, there are some people who <u>don't see no</u> reason to keep them
35

<u>except</u> for food or work. These animals, called pets, can affect us deeply.
36

They offer the <u>more rare</u> kind of affection: unconditional love. Furthermore,
37

when we <u>are petting</u> animals, we are making positive changes in our bodies
38

by lowering blood pressure and releasing soothing hormones in the brain.

For Numbers 34 through 38, decide which answer choice shows correct usage.

34. *a* are having

    b will have had

    c have had

    d Correct as it is

35. *a* don't never see

    b never see no

    c don't see any

    d Correct as it is

36. *a* accept

    b accepting

    c excepting

    d Correct as it is

37. *a* rarer

    b rarest

    c most rarest

    d Correct as it is

38. *a* petted

    b would pet

    c were petting

    d Correct as it is

SENTENCE FORMATION

A *sentence* is a group of words that provides a complete idea. A sentence does not have to be long, but it must contain a *subject* and a *predicate*.

Sentence Formation includes subskills, such as Sentence Recognition and Sentence Combining.

Look at these examples. Find the sentence in each group that is complete *and* shows the correct capitalization and punctuation.

EXAMPLE	ANSWER
a The ball high in the air.	• **Answer *a* is not** correct. This sentence has no verb.
b Three points were scored.	• **Answer *b* is correct.** This is a complete sentence with a subject and a verb.
c Cheered for the home team.	• **Answer *c* is not** correct. This sentence has no subject.
d Having run across the field.	• **Answer *d* is not** correct. This is an incomplete sentence because it has no subject.

This graphic illustrates how a sentence is formed:

| must have a *subject* and a *predicate* | **A Sentence** | should *express the idea clearly* |

should carry *proper punctuation*

EXAMPLE	ANSWER
a Sitting in the waiting room reading a magazine.	• **Answer *a* is not** correct. This phrase does not give a complete idea.
b New dental techniques that are fast and painless.	• **Answer *b* is not** correct. This sentence is incomplete. The idea is not finished.
c Visiting a dentist regularly can help prevent tooth decay.	• **Answer *c* is** correct. This is a complete sentence.
d My dentist is Dr. Montoya her office isn't far from where I live.	• **Answer *d* is not** correct. This is a compound sentence with two subjects and two verbs. A semicolon is needed between the words *Dr. Montoya* and *her*.

Choose the sentence in each group that is complete and shows the correct capitalization *and* punctuation.
First, try Numbers 1 and 2 for practice.

1. *a* When we visit the city next week, we'll see a movie and go out to dinner.

   b Everyone met at Debbie's house then we took Leo's van into the city.

   c A few days off work to stay home and relax.

   d Planning to celebrate the holiday with friends.

   ANSWER *a* is correct. This is a complete sentence.

2. *a* Department meetings starting on time.

   b Doing the most important things first.

   c As a salesperson, you must be able to manage your time effectively.

   d You should work your assigned hours take breaks only as scheduled.

   ANSWER *c* is correct. This is a complete sentence.

Now you are ready to do more problems. The answers to the problems in this section can be found in the back of this workbook.

This graphic helps you remember what a subject and a predicate are.

| **Subject** { | A person
A place
A thing | **Predicate** { | Tells what the subject is doing
Describes the subject
Identifies the subject |

Joan *is my wife.*
(subject)

Joan, my wife, **works with me in the lab***.*
(predicate)

Sometimes, two sentences can be combined into one to create a better, clearer sentence. Look at the following example:

| *The cab driver maneuvered his way through the traffic.* | *The cab driver maneuvered expertly.* |

The cab driver expertly maneuvered his way through the traffic.

For Numbers 3 through 6, read the underlined sentences. Choose the sentence that *best* combines those sentences into one.

3. The word processing equipment is new.

   It makes producing complicated documents easy.

   a The word processing equipment makes producing new, complicated documents easy.

   b The new word processing equipment makes producing complicated documents easy.

   c The word processing equipment, producing complicated documents, is new and easy.

   d The word processing equipment makes producing complicated documents easy and new.

4. Peter ate his lunch at the cafeteria.

   The cafeteria has recently opened.

   a Peter ate his lunch at the recently opened cafeteria.

   b Recently opened, Peter ate his lunch at the cafeteria.

   c The cafeteria has opened and is where Peter recently ate his lunch.

   d Peter ate his lunch at the cafeteria, and the cafeteria has recently opened.

 Reminder Modifiers that combine two sentences should *not* change the meaning of the original sentences.

5. I bought a winter jacket last week.

I haven't worn it yet.

a I bought a winter jacket last week, but I haven't worn it yet.

b Since I bought a winter jacket last week, I haven't worn it yet.

c I haven't worn the winter jacket yet, because I bought it last week.

d Having bought a winter jacket last week, I haven't worn it yet.

6. The members of the team are anxious to show their training level.

The members of the team are confident of winning the match.

a The members of the team are anxious to show their training level, as they are confident of winning the match.

b Anxious to show their training level, the members of the team are, therefore, confident of winning the match.

c Since the members of the team are confident of winning the match, they are anxious to show their training level.

d The members of the team are anxious to show their training level and are confident of winning the match.

For Numbers 7 and 8, read the underlined sentences. Choose the sentence that *best* combines those sentences into one.

7. Very upset, Angela pushed the cart down the aisle.

   Angela pushed the cart toward the check-out stand.

   a Angela, who pushed the cart down the aisle very upset, pushed it toward the check-out stand.

   b Angela pushed the cart down the aisle, and very upset she pushed the cart toward the check-out stand.

   c Very upset pushing the cart down the aisle, Angela pushed the cart toward the check-out stand.

   d Angela, who was very upset, pushed the cart down the aisle toward the check-out stand.

8. The auto mechanic didn't see the customer.

   The customer was hurrying through the garage doorway.

   a Because the auto mechanic didn't see him, the customer was hurrying through the garage doorway.

   b The auto mechanic didn't see the customer, and the customer was hurrying through the garage doorway.

   c The auto mechanic didn't see the customer who was hurrying through the garage doorway.

   d While the customer was hurrying through the garage doorway, the auto mechanic didn't see him.

For Numbers 9 through 13, choose the sentence in each group that is complete *and* shows the correct capitalization and punctuation.

9. *a* We prefer eating homemade food than to go to a fast food restaurant.

   b She is anxious to drop off the diet and being able to eat what she likes.

   c When I look through our photo album, I recall the holiday time our family spent together.

   d When Tad goes back home, he enjoys home cooking, seeing old friends, and is relaxed.

10. *a* We heard that stormy weather was ahead on the weather forecast.

   b I drove home after waiting three hours for the rain to subside.

   c Philip listened to the story about the snowstorm, bored and a little sleepy.

   d Did you find your umbrella yesterday when it started to rain in the back of the closet?

When listing several actions in a sentence, be sure to use the same verb tense for each action. For example: *We like **watching** movies, **going** to the theater, and **listening** to live music.*

11. *a* I rented a video about carpentry after work.

  b She was lulled to sleep by the soft music lying on the couch.

  c Taking a shortcut home from work, I discovered a new video store.

  d He enjoyed his soda as he watched the movie filled with ice.

12. *a* In the past, business was regarded as the ability to preserve customers.

  b Today's modern business colleges presently teach essential, basic topics.

  c The main primary focus of her business is to offer timely up-to-date investment advice.

  d Many people think that being a good business person is something you are born with at birth.

Reminder

A *misplaced modifier* can confuse the meaning of a sentence. Be sure to place modifiers as close as possible to the word(s) they modify. For example:

I see more housing developments *driving through our city every day.*

Driving through our city every day, I see more housing developments.

13. *a* Secretaries often, generally, schedule meetings, notify committee members, and take minutes.

   b The committee members gather together, and assemble in meetings every week.

   c Each minute offers a detailed account, a particular description, of the main items discussed.

   d The manager informed the staff of all the new changes to be made effective the following month.

Avoid repetition of words, phrases, or ideas in the same sentence.

PARAGRAPH DEVELOPMENT

A paragraph is a group of sentences that are written about a single thought or idea. A good paragraph has a topic sentence that gives the main idea, followed by other sentences that support that idea. For good *paragraph development*, stay focused on a topic or idea and exclude unnecessary or irrelevant information.

Paragraph Development includes subskills, such as Topic Sentence, Supporting Sentence, and Sequence.

In this example, the paragraph below is missing a topic sentence. Read the supporting sentences and find the *best* topic sentence for the paragraph.

EXAMPLE	ANSWER

EXAMPLE

_____ This includes the study of the physical and chemical properties of the water, sea plants, and animals, as well as the geology of the seabed. This relatively new discipline has produced enormous changes in our understanding of the submarine world.

a   Oceanography can involve exploring deep water caves for unknown life.

b   Oceanography is a young science that has led to important discoveries in its field.

c   Oceanography is the exploration and scientific study of the ocean and its phenomena.

d   Oceanography has changed the way people see our world and its preservation.

ANSWER

- **Answers a, b,** and **d** are **not** correct. Although related to the subject, they do not fit best in the blank provided.

- **Answer c** is correct. This sentence best explains the topic developed in the sentences following it.

Reminder

The *topic sentence* provides the main idea of the paragraph. It gives a general idea of how the rest of the sentences in the paragraph might be written.

Now look at the following paragraphs. For each paragraph, find the *best* topic sentence. First, try Numbers 1 and 2 for practice.

1. _____ They are thoroughly washed before being submitted to a high-pressure steam cleaning to kill the bacteria. Then they are sterilized again before being sent to surgery, where they are handled with great care. This procedure has prevented many infections.

    a Biotechnicians are responsible for cleaning and sterilizing surgical instruments.

    b Surgical instruments undergo a complicated cleaning process.

    c Sterilization eliminates organisms that can cause infection.

    d The cleaning process in surgery is extremely important and should be done with great care.

ANSWER *b* is correct. This sentence presents the topic that is developed in the paragraph.

2. _____ Today you will find women using a welder's torch and wearing a hardhat. They are often seen climbing utility poles or operating heavy equipment. In contrast, men can be found working as nurses and secretaries.

    a Women can do almost any kind of work they choose.

    b Most people want jobs that are personally satisfying and that pay well.

    c Titles of jobs have changed so that they no longer imply that only men are doing them.

    d No longer are jobs strictly "man's work" or "woman's work."

ANSWER *d* is correct. This sentence presents the topic that is developed in the paragraph.

Now you are ready to do more problems. The answers to the problems in this section can be found in the back of this workbook.

Read the following paragraphs. For Numbers 3 and 4, find the sentence that *best* completes each paragraph.

3. When it is time for a patient to be discharged from a hospital, the nurse first schedules any necessary follow-up appointments. _____ Finally, the discharge papers are signed, and the patient may leave.

    a   Frequently, patients are anxious to leave the hospital.

    b   Before leaving, the patient should be checked out by a doctor.

    c   Once at home, the patient may call the hospital with questions.

    d   Then the nurse may arrange for home care for the patient.

Pay attention to words such as *first, next,* and *then.* They indicate the *sequence,* or logical order, of events.

4. Before Mara paints a house, she pressure washes the area to be painted. _____ Next, she scrapes away any remaining loose paint. Then, she applies a coat of primer to all exposed wood and metal. After taping off the trim and window areas, she is ready to apply the paint. Finally, after painting the trim, the project is completed.

   a Sometimes she finds that two coats of paint are necessary.

   b Painting the trim is frequently the most time-consuming task.

   c She is very careful to avoid window and door areas that may leak.

   d Primer also must be applied to dark areas that will require lighter paint.

Good paragraphs show *development of ideas* and a *connection* between those ideas, creating a smooth flow of information.

For Numbers 5 and 6, read the following passages.
Then, find the sentence that *best* completes each paragraph.

5. Major league baseball teams are now using computers to help make important decisions. Traditional statistics, such as batting averages and earned-run averages, are now supplemented with strategic data never before available to team managers. For instance, the computer can show how a team's players will perform in a certain park, against a given pitcher, on artificial turf, or with various runners on base. _____

   a Thus, in some ways the manager's job has become much more complicated.

   b Thereafter, the manager's decisions are often the result of a complex set of factors.

   c Otherwise, the modern manager's job involves more than acting on hunches and simple percentages.

   d For example, today's managers must sort and interpret this information quickly and accurately to make crucial decisions.

Reminder

Transition words serve to connect ideas within a paragraph or to make a transition between two different ideas.

6. Tourism is a great economic resource for many countries. _____ The improvement in communications and the accessibility to different methods of travel has increased the amount of people traveling. Business people as well as tourists are now enjoying the benefits of this prosperous industry.

   a Nevertheless, for some countries it is the main financial resource.

   b In fact, for some countries it is the main financial resource.

   c For instance, for some countries it is the main financial resource.

   d Therefore, for some countries it is the main financial resource.

For Numbers 7 and 8, read each topic sentence and each set of supporting sentences. Select the sentences that *best* support each topic sentence.

7. Most companies are made up of several departments.

   a They usually have departments for shipping, human resources, and customer service. Many companies also have marketing, finance, and computer-related departments.

   b Each floor may be home to a completely different company than the floor above or below it. Buildings like these are usually found only in large cities.

   c This department deals with issues such as payroll, benefits, and hiring. It is a key department in ensuring that employees are treated fairly.

   d In cases like these, new managers are promoted, hired, or moved to a different part of the company. These moves often take a long time to implement and even longer to adjust to.

8. There are a variety of benefits offered by modern businesses.

   a Many of these employees work long hours and then go home to care for families. Other people have commitments such as school or volunteering that limit their free time.

   b Some workers go to work early in order to leave earlier or go to work late and leave late. Other employees may work long hours in order to work a shorter week.

   c Problems between coworkers are usually handled by the employees' manager. If the problem is between a manager and his or her employee, human resources usually handles the incident.

   d Carpooling and flexible hours are popular benefits offered by today's companies. On-site day care, money investment programs, and college tuition reimbursement are also common benefits.

For Numbers 9 and 10, read the paragraph and look for the sentence that does *not* belong.

9. **1.** After leaving a job, you may have more of a guarantee of continued health care coverage than when you were employed. **2.** Health care insurance is one of many employment benefits offered by companies. **3.** While you work, your employer can change or cancel your insurance at any time. **4.** If you quit your job or are fired, however, you have the legal right to continued protection for eighteen months, although you will probably have to pay the premiums yourself.

 a Sentence 1

 b Sentence 2

 c Sentence 3

 d Sentence 4

10. **1.** Motorists who drive older cars designed to run on leaded gasoline face a dilemma. **2.** Leaded gasoline is difficult to find in most parts of the country, while unleaded gas, although readily available, may not provide the lubricating properties necessary to protect an older engine. **3.** Most cars manufactured after 1975 have been designed to run on unleaded fuel. **4.** One alternative is to use a fuel additive with unleaded gasoline; the additive will act as a lubricant in place of lead.

 a Sentence 1

 b Sentence 2

 c Sentence 3

 d Sentence 4

All answer choices will be *related* to the topic presented, but one should stand out as being either out of sequence or out of place in the paragraph.

CAPITALIZATION

Capitalization refers to the rules used for mixing capital letters (A, B, C, D) and lowercase letters (a, b, c, d) in writing. Proper nouns (names of people, places, holidays, days of the week, etc.) always begin with a capital letter. Other words may be capitalized if they come at the beginning of a sentence or are part of a title.

Capitalization includes subskills, such as First Word, Proper Nouns, and Title of Work.

Read the following examples. Look at the underlined words. Find the answer choice that is written correctly for each underlined part.

EXAMPLE	ANSWER
John Steinbeck, the author of <u>*the Grapes of wrath,*</u> received the Nobel Prize for Literature in 1962.	• **Answer *a*** is **not** correct. The words *grapes* and *wrath* should be capitalized.
a *The grapes of wrath,*	• **Answer *b*** is correct. This is a compound title of a work and all the words <u>except the preposition</u> *of* should be capitalized.
b *The Grapes of Wrath,*	
c *the grapes of Wrath,*	• **Answer *c*** is **not** correct. The words *the* and *grapes* should be capitalized.
d Correct as it is	• **Answer *d*** is **not** correct. The article *the* should be capitalized as well as the noun *wrath*.

EXAMPLE	ANSWER

We camped in <u>Yellowstone national Park.</u>

a Yellowstone National Park.

b yellowstone National Park.

c yellowstone national park.

d Correct as it is

- **Answer *a*** is correct. The complete name should be capitalized.

- **Answer *b*** is **not** correct. The word *yellowstone* should be capitalized.

- **Answer *c*** is **not** correct. The three words should be capitalized.

- **Answer *d*** is **not** correct. The word *national* should be capitalized.

For each of the following sentences, select the answer choice that shows the correct capitalization.
First, try Numbers 1 and 2 for practice.

1.   My cousin Dave auditioned for a part in the play *inherit the wind*.

   a   *Inherit the wind.*

   b   *inherit The Wind.*

   c   *Inherit the Wind.*

   d   Correct as it is

ANSWER **c** is correct. This is the correct way of writing the name of the play.

2.   Jaime received a degree in Computer Science from the University of georgia.

   a   university of georgia.

   b   University of Georgia.

   c   university of Georgia.

   d   Correct as it is

ANSWER **b** is correct. This is the correct way of writing the name of the university.

Now you are ready to do more problems. The answers to the problems in this section can be found in the back of this workbook.

We capitalize words to let readers know that a word represents something very specific. Names of places *(Palm Beach, Hong Kong)* or titles of works *(David Copperfield, Treasure Island)* are always capitalized.

For Numbers 3 and 4, select the answer choice that shows the correct capitalization for the underlined words.

3. Mark read _A Tale of two cities_ by Charles Dickens.

   a *A Tale of two Cities*

   b *A tale of two cities*

   c *A Tale of Two Cities*

   d Correct as it is

4. His plane will leave for <u>South America</u> in two hours.

   a south America

   b South america

   c south america

   d Correct as it is

Articles and prepositions are not capitalized in titles of works or place names:
Stephen Crane wrote The Red Badge of Courage.
*Sheila has just returned from **the** United Kingdom.*
An exception is when the articles or prepositions *start* the title or name: ***Of** Mice and Men*.

> **Now, look at Numbers 5 and 6.**
> **Rewrite each sentence, using the correct capitalization.**

5. Last week I was in north Miami beach. I had a wonderful vacation!

   _____

6. Shakespeare not only wrote tragedies and historical novels, but also comedies like *much ado about nothing*.

   _____

   _____

Reminder

An article is a word that specifies whether a noun is definite or indefinite, such as the, a, an.
A preposition is a part of speech which indicates a connection between two other parts of speech, such as to, with, by, or from.

NOTES

PUNCTUATION

Writers use *punctuation* to separate words into sentences and to help make meanings clear. There are many punctuation marks, including periods (.), question marks (?), exclamation marks (!), commas (,), and quotation marks (" "). The use or non-use of punctuation marks can affect the meaning of a sentence.

Punctuation includes subskills, such as End Marks and Commas.

Read the sample sentences and decide which punctuation mark, if any, is needed.

EXAMPLE	ANSWER
Haven't you seen that movie before *a* , *b* ? *c* ! *d* None	• **Answer *a* is not** correct. No comma is necessary in this sentence. • **Answer *b* is** correct. This is a question; therefore, it needs a question mark. • **Answer *c* is not** correct. This is not an exclamation and does not need an exclamation mark. • **Answer *d* is not** correct. This sentence needs a question mark.

EXAMPLE	ANSWER
She lost her wallet, the one you gave her last year, while she was jogging.	• **Answer *a* is not correct.** This is not an exclamation, so an exclamation mark is not needed.
a !	• **Answer *b* is not correct.** No semicolon is required in this sentence.
b ;	• **Answer *c* is not correct.** This is not a question, so a question mark is not needed.
c ?	• **Answer *d* is correct.** The expression *the one you gave her last year* is providing an explanation and is correctly separated by commas.
d None	

Read the following sentences. Select the appropriate punctuation mark, if needed.
First, try Numbers 1 and 2 for practice.

1. Is it better to use paper or plastic bags

    a ?

    b .

    c !

    d None

    ANSWER *a* is correct. This is a question; therefore, a question mark is needed.

2. We planted that tree the one by the fence, last year.

    a .

    b ;

    c ,

    d None

    ANSWER *c* is correct. A comma is needed after the word *tree*. The expression *the one by the fence* is an appositive, an explanatory phrase, and should be separated by commas.

Now you are ready to do more problems. The answers to the problems in this section can be found in the back of this workbook.

 Each punctuation mark has its own meaning and communicates a different message to a reader. A period (.) signals the end of a complete thought. A comma (,) signals a pause or a change of thought. A question mark (?) signals that a question has been asked. An exclamation mark (!) signals excitement, emphasis, or emotion.

For Numbers 3 through 5, identify the sentence that is complete *and* punctuated correctly.

3. *a* Which way is Fourth Street?

   b Here come the fire engines?

   c Where is the fire hydrant.

   d Watch out for the wet cement,

4. *a* By the way have you seen María lately?

   b No in fact, I haven't seen her for ages.

   c Well, I suppose she must be busy with her new baby.

   d Oh I didn't even know she was expecting another one.

5. *a* The parade, which will be down Main Street begins at noon.

   b Several participants, many of whom were children, dressed in costumes.

   c The Wildcats the local high school band drew the loudest cheers.

   d Diana Contreras the city mayor, announced the winner of the best float.

Use commas in these cases:
- appositives (*My sister, **the younger one,** just got married.*)
- items in a series (*We need **bread, milk,** and **cheese**.*)
- introductory elements (***As I was saying,** I've never been to Mexico.*)

For Numbers 6 through 8, identify the sentence that is complete *and* punctuated correctly.

6. *a* Some people I think have more compassion than others.

  b The money for the most part, will be donated to homeless shelters in the area.

  c The purpose of the organization, in fact is to raise money for the homeless.

  d Very few, if any, choose such a difficult lifestyle.

7. *a* A money market account for instance is usually a safe investment.

  b Investing in stocks and bonds on the other hand, can be quite risky.

  c Real estate values, in my opinion will remain stable over the next few years.

  d I don't need a mathematician, however, to calculate the growth of my bank account.

8. *a* The teller took my money counted it sealed the bill, and gave it to me.

  b When I get on the bus, I like to read a magazine, a newspaper, or, a book.

  c My Friday errands include going to the bank, the dry cleaners, and the grocery store.

  d Let's see the movie you mentioned on Wednesday Thursday or Saturday.

Reminder

Within a sentence, you may find two different ideas. A semicolon (;) should be placed between them. For example: *André has fought some terrible fires; still, he loves his job. The city needs another fire station; the existing station is not adequate for the city's size.*

The following sentences are missing punctuation marks. For Numbers 9 through 12, rewrite each sentence with the correct punctuation.

9. Ben's bags are all packed he'll be on his way to Toledo this morning.

_____

10. Exercising regularly is good for one's health nevertheless, few people exercise enough.

_____

11. Unfortunately I was in the elevator when the electricity went out.

_____

12. The apartment is furnished with a stove, a refrigerator a table, and two chairs.

_____

WRITING CONVENTIONS

Writing conventions are the rules and customs we follow when writing. These conventions act as an important code for readers. Rules regarding when to use an apostrophe ('), how to punctuate quotations (" "), and the proper format for addresses, business letters, and personal letters are all *writing conventions*.

Writing Conventions includes subskills, such as Quotation Marks, Apostrophes, and Letter Parts.

Look at the example.
Select the appropriate punctuation mark, if needed.

EXAMPLE	ANSWER
Ray shouted, That pan is hot!"	• **Answer *a*** is **not** correct. This sentence does not need a period.
a .	
b "	• **Answer *b*** is correct. The expression *That pan is hot!* is a quotation and needs a beginning quotation mark before *That*.
c ?	• **Answer *c*** is **not** correct. This is not a question; therefore, a question mark is not needed.
d None	• **Answer *d*** is **not** correct. This sentence does require punctuation, so *None* is not a correct answer.

Look at the example. Find the sentence that is complete *and* punctuated correctly.

EXAMPLE	ANSWER
a She waited nervously in the dentists office.	• **Answer *a* is not** correct. This sentence needs a possessive form; therefore, the correct spelling is *dentist's*.
b Two years' have gone by since your last checkup.	• **Answer *b* is not** correct. The word *years* refers to the plural, so an apostrophe is not needed.
c Claude had a toothache and was'nt getting much sleep.	• **Answer *c* is not** correct. The apostrophe should be placed between the *n* and the *t*.
d The receptionist entered all the patients' names into the computer.	• **Answer *d* is correct.** *Patients* is in the plural form; therefore, the possessive is indicated with an apostrophe after the *s*.

Decide which punctuation mark, if any, is needed in these sentences. First, try Numbers 1 and 2 for practice.

1. "Wait, said Maura, "I need a ride to the grocery store."

   a " "

   b .

   c ,

   d None

   ANSWER *a* is correct. A quotation mark is needed before the word *said*.

2. "I wonder," said Ellie hopefully, "whether the air conditioner will be working soon."

   a ,

   b ?

   c ;

   d None

   ANSWER *d* is correct. This sentence does not require additional punctuation marks.

Now you are ready to do more problems. The answers to the problems in this section can be found in the back of this workbook.

 Look at the explanatory words (he *said*, she *hollered*, they *asked*) to determine what punctuation is needed for a quotation.

Now, complete Numbers 3 and 4. Examine the following groups of sentences. Find the sentence in each group that is punctuated correctly.

3.　*a*　Did you say that this seat is your's or mine?

　　b　Aren't those seat's reserved for Pedro and Elsa?

　　c　Why don't you sit down and make yourselve's comfortable?

　　d　Isn't the guest of honor's seat at the head of the table?

4.　*a*　"Wait a minute!" I said loudly, "I'd like to see the manager."

　　b　"How can they stay in business," asked Abel, "when they're so rude to their customers."

　　c　"May I speak with your Client Service Department," I asked the sales clerk?

　　d　The manager said, "It is not our policy to give refunds".

An apostrophe should only be used if a word is a contraction (*I **can't** find my keys*) or if a word is showing possession (*My **mother's** new sofa is made of leather*). When a noun is both plural *and* possessive and ends in *s*, place the apostrophe *after* the final *s: The **dogs'** barking kept me awake. The **students'** books were in their lockers.*

Read this letter that Constance wrote to her dentist.
Identify any errors in the underlined parts.

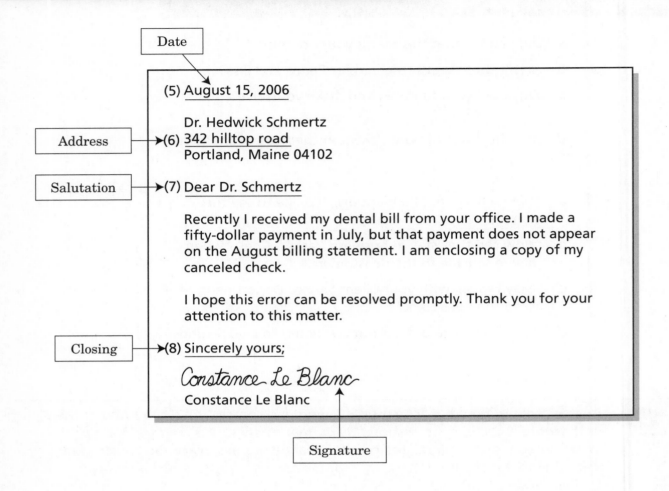

Date

(5) August 15, 2006

Dr. Hedwick Schmertz
Address
(6) 342 hilltop road
Portland, Maine 04102

Salutation
(7) Dear Dr. Schmertz

Recently I received my dental bill from your office. I made a
fifty-dollar payment in July, but that payment does not appear
on the August billing statement. I am enclosing a copy of my
canceled check.

I hope this error can be resolved promptly. Thank you for your
attention to this matter.

Closing
(8) Sincerely yours;

Constance Le Blanc
Constance Le Blanc

Signature

Reminder

Writing the address
correctly on an envelope
will help your letter arrive
safely.

Now, for Numbers 5 through 8, find the correct format for each underlined part of the letter.

5. *a*   august 15 2006

   b   August, 15 2006

   c   august 15, 2006

   d   Correct as it is

6. *a*   342 Hilltop road

   b   342 Hilltop Road

   c   342 hilltop Road

   d   Correct as it is

7. *a*   Dear Dr. Schmertz:

   b   Dear Dr. Schmertz;

   c   dear Dr. Schmertz

   d   Correct as it is

8. *a*   Sincerely yours,

   b   sincerely yours,

   c   Sincerely Yours;

   d   Correct as it is

Read this thank-you note that Pat wrote. Look at the underlined parts.

(9) <u>May 30 2006</u>

Mrs. Elin Wong
(10) <u>112 byron st.</u>
San Diego, CA 92116

(11) <u>Dear Mrs. Wong</u>

Thank you very much for speaking at the Emergency Medical
(12) <u>Technicianses</u> Workshop. Your words were timely and appropriate. You
began, "Is there anybody in this room who doubts the urgent need for
(13) good emergency <u>technicians</u>"? Your question silenced the room!

I am looking forward to reading your new book.

(14) <u>Very Truly Yours,</u>

Pat Robert
Pat Robert

Now, for Numbers 9 through 14, write the correct format for each underlined part in the letter.

9. _____

10. _____

11. _____

12. _____

13. _____

14. _____

VOWEL

Vowels are letters of the alphabet which represent certain sounds, depending on how they are combined with other letters. The letters *a, e, i, o, u,* and *y* (sometimes) are vowels. Each vowel stands for several different (spoken) sounds.

Vowel includes subskills, such as Short Vowel, Long Vowel, Schwa, and R-Controlled Vowel.

For these examples, find the word that is spelled correctly.

EXAMPLE	ANSWER
The farmer clipped the sheep's _____. a fleice b fleace c fleece d fliece	• **Answers a, b,** and **d** are **not** correct. They all contain the wrong spelling of the long e sound. • **Answer c** is correct. The long e sound is spelled *ee: fleece.*

EXAMPLE	ANSWER
After the accident, his driver's license was _____. a revoked b revoaked c revolked d revowked	• **Answer a** is correct. The long o is spelled *o: re-voked.* • **Answers b, c,** and **d** are **not** correct. They all contain the wrong spelling of the long o sound.

**Choose the word that is spelled correctly.
First, try Numbers 1 and 2 for practice.**

1. My friend brought back a _____ of her trip.

    a soovenir

    b suvenir

    c souvenir

    d suovenir

    ANSWER *c* is correct. The long *u* sound is spelled *ou: sou-ven-ir.*

2. The judge dismissed the jury from the _____.

    a preceedings

    b proceedings

    c praceedings

    d priceedings

    ANSWER *b* is correct. The long *o* sound is spelled *o: pro-ceed-ings.*

**Now you are ready to do more problems. The answers to the
problems in this section can be found in the back of this workbook.**

For Numbers 3 and 4, look at each sentence group. One of the underlined words is *not* spelled correctly. Find the misspelled word and write the correct spelling.

3. These plants belong to a different <u>catigory</u>.

    Today's dinner has a <u>charitable</u> purpose.

    I have some <u>nominal</u> shares of this company.

    He has <u>acquired</u> some experience since his first job.

    _____

4. She came up with an <u>ingenious</u> solution.

    The strong <u>disagreement</u> they showed affected everybody.

    <u>Idially</u> the children should go first in the race.

    The rule will have an <u>immediate</u> effect.

    _____

 Vowels can be long, like the *a* in *baby,* or short, like the *a* in *bat.* Some vowel sounds aren't as distinct, such as the *a* in the word *sofa.*

For Numbers 5 through 9, read the following sentences. Choose the word that is spelled correctly.

5. I couldn't _____ of a way to fix the problem.

   a conceive

   b conceeve

   c conceave

   d concieve

6. The public laughed at the _____ speech made by the comedian.

   a ridiculous

   b rideculous

   c riduculous

   d ridoculous

7. The new vice president will _____ to make the company successful.

   a endevor

   b endehvor

   c endeivor

   d endeavor

Do not rely simply on *sounding out* words. Use your memory of spelling rules, too.

Read the following sentences.
Choose the word that is spelled correctly.

8. The _____ word list is several pages long.

   a   cumulutive

   b   cumulative

   c   cumulitive

   d   cumulotive

9. A dog with a hat on seemed _____
   to me.

   a   ludicrus

   b   ludicrous

   c   ludecrous

   d   ludecrus

The *schwa* sound is an unstressed vowel
sound. It can be spelled with any vowel, as
well as several different combinations of
vowels: *rider, oppose, anonymous, caution*.

The underlined word in each sentence is *not* spelled correctly.
For Numbers 10 through 13, write the correct spelling.

10. Claudia had to <u>manouver</u> her car around the garbage can.

_____

11. Pat is a member of a scientific <u>instatute</u>.

_____

12. My sister is a <u>vetirinarian</u>.

_____

13. Our project underwent a <u>fundumental</u> change.

_____

CONSONANT

Consonants are letters or combinations of letters, such as **f, b,** and **ch,** that represent certain sounds. Using the wrong consonant can change the meaning of a word completely.

Consonant includes subskills, such as **Variant Spelling, Silent Letter,** and **Double Letter.**

For these examples, find the word that is spelled correctly.

EXAMPLE	ANSWER
The tree's _____ is clearly visible in the moonlight. *a* silouete *b* silouette *c* silhouette *d* silhouete	• **Answers a, b,** and **d** are **not** correct. These words are not spelled correctly. • **Answer c** is correct. The *h* is silent: *sil-**hou**-ette*.

Reminder

Silent letters are letters that appear in a word's spelling but are not pronounced when the word is spoken.

EXAMPLE	ANSWER
Her collection of unusual _____ is displayed on a shelf. *a* niknaks *b* niknacks *c* knicknacks *d* knickknacks	• **Answers a, b,** and **c** are **not** correct. Each shows a misspelling of the word. • **Answer d** is correct. The *k* is silent: **knick-knacks**.

Look at the following sentences. Choose the word that is spelled correctly. First, try Numbers 1 and 2 for practice.

1. Sarah had _____ about the schedule.

   a quams

   b qualms

   c quawms

   d quoms

   ANSWER *b* is correct. The *l* is silent: *qualms*.

2. My cousin Bob is studying to be a _____.

   a sychologist

   b cychologist

   c psychologist

   d scychologist

   ANSWER *c* is correct. The *p* is silent: *psy-cho-lo-gist*.

Now you are ready to do more problems. The answers to the problems in this section can be found in the back of this workbook.

Sometimes consonants are silent, but their placement in a word creates its unique meaning, such as the silent *s* in the word *island*.

Reminder

Consonant sounds can be spelled in various ways. For example, the *j* sound in the word *juggle* is the same sound as the *g* in the word *huge*, or the *dg* in the word *judge*.

The J sound

ju**gg**le

hu**g**e

ju**dg**e

For Numbers 3 through 5, find the word that is spelled correctly.

3. Some herbs have a _____ odor.

    a pungunt

    b punjunt

    c punjent

    d pungent

4. Celia is _____ and will often send herself dozens of flowers.

    a impechuous

    b impetchuous

    c impetuous

    d impecuous

5. Amy was _____ to her job.

    a comited

    b commited

    c comitted

    d committed

Tip

Sometimes consonants are *doubled* when a longer consonant sound is needed, such as in the words *jelly* and *supper*. Pay close attention to the sound of each syllable to see where the double letters are: *jel-ly, sup-per*.

In each sentence, the underlined word is *not* spelled correctly. For Numbers 6 through 8, write the correct spelling.

6. I didn't like the <u>roufness</u> of the cloth.

_____

7. His new apartment certainly is <u>spatious</u>.

_____

8. My <u>predecesor</u> left me a detailed schedule.

_____

For Numbers 9 and 10, one of the underlined words is *not* spelled correctly. Find the misspelled word and write the correct spelling.

9. The <u>access</u> has been restricted to members only.

The final <u>acceptance</u> depends on the board members.

Owing to <u>incesant</u> inquiries, an information desk has been opened.

Their words were very <u>offensive</u>, although they offered an apology later.

_____

10. We enjoyed the <u>legendary</u> tales of Robin Hood.

They were placed in a very <u>stratejic</u> position.

This text is overcrowded with <u>adjectives</u>.

My <u>knowledge</u> on this subject is very limited.

_____

STRUCTURAL UNIT

Structural units are parts of words. Sometimes it is easier to spell a word if you break it into its structural units, or parts. Prefixes, roots, and suffixes are types of structural units that make up words such as:

> **un-** + ***kind*** + **-ly** = ***unkindly***
> *prefix*   *root*   *suffix*   *word*

Structural Unit includes subskills, such as Homonym, Similar Word Part, Root, and Suffix.

Look at the example.
Choose the word that is spelled correctly.

EXAMPLE	ANSWER
The noise of planes flying overhead is a continual _____. *a* annoyance *b* annoiance *c* annoance *d* annoyiance	• **Answer *a*** is correct. It combines the root word *annoy* with the suffix *-ance*. It is not necessary to change or drop the ending of the root word. • **Answers *b, c,*** and ***d*** are **not** spelled correctly.

Look at the example.
Choose the word that is spelled correctly.

EXAMPLE	ANSWER

The _____ continued based on the amount of complaints received.

a investigatetion

b investigetion

c investigateion

d investigation

• **Answers *a*, *b*,** and ***c*** are **not** spelled correctly.

• **Answer *d*** is correct. The root word *investigate* drops the final *e* when adding the suffix *-ion*.

Sometimes it is necessary to change the spelling of a root word when adding a suffix.

Reminder

Choose the word that is spelled correctly.
First, try Numbers 1 and 2 for practice.

1. The _____ between them is strong.

   a resemblance

   b resemblence

   c resemblunce

   d resembleance

   ANSWER *a* is correct. The root word is *resemble* and the suffix is *-ance*.
   The e is dropped when the suffix is added: *re-sem-bl**ance***.

2. The _____ wrote an article about beetles.

   a entomologyst

   b entomologist

   c entomologyist

   d entomologiste

   ANSWER *b* is correct. The root word is *entomology* and the suffix is *-ist*.
   The y is dropped when the suffix is added: *en-to-mol-o-**gist***.

Now you are ready to do more problems. The answers to the problems in this section can be found in the back of this workbook.

Often the structural unit of a word consists of a root word with a part added. For example, if the root word *grant* is combined with the suffix *-ed*, the past tense verb *granted* is created.

For Numbers 3 and 4, choose the word that is spelled correctly.

3. _____ of this product are making huge profits.

   a Distributars

   b Distributers

   c Distributors

   d Distributurs

4. The _____ always wants to find the best product.

   a consumar

   b consumer

   c consumir

   d consumor

Break words into syllables to discover their structural units. Look for breaks between root words and common suffixes or prefixes:

Prefix Root Suffix

smiling

unkind

proportionate

For Numbers 5 through 8, choose the word that is spelled correctly to *best* complete the sentence.

5. Even a light touch can trigger a car's alarm _____.

   a sencer

   b censor

   c sensor

   d cencer

6. The mood of the _____ was changing.

   a populus

   b populuce

   c populous

   d populace

7. My friend was the _____ of a large cash award.

   a recipeint

   b recipaint

   c recipient

   d recipiant

8. Her _____ was obvious.

   a impatiense

   b impatiance

   c impatience

   d impatianse

Reminder

Homonyms are words that *sound* the same but have different *meanings* depending on the way they are spelled.

For Numbers 9 and 10, the underlined word is *not* spelled correctly. Write the correct spelling.

9. He showed his speaking <u>capabilaty</u> during the debate.

_____

10. At the crowd's <u>insistance</u>, Anna sang another song.

_____

For Numbers 11 and 12, one of the underlined words is *not* spelled correctly to *best* complete the sentence. Find the misspelled word and write the correct spelling.

11. I led that black horse by its <u>bridal</u>.
    The nation was consolidated during his <u>reign</u>.
    This is a <u>complementary</u> booklet for the main text.
    We were invaded by an agreeable pine <u>scent</u>.

_____

12. He thought the <u>requirements</u> for the job were not well defined.
    The <u>Fertility</u> Research Institute has come up with new discoveries.
    Knowing the public's <u>acceptance</u>, we had no doubt about its success.
    Suzanne ignored the <u>existance</u> of strict regulations on this matter.

_____

Some *parts* of words sound similar. Pronounce the spellings clearly to distinguish between similar word parts.

Tip

Answer Key

Question	Answer	READING: Interpret Graphic Information, Level A
3	*a*	There is an hour and a half difference between Onslow and Darwin.
4	*c*	This map would most likely be found in an **encyclopedia.**
5	*b*	*Flamenco guitar playing: a method for beginners* is an instructional guide on how to play flamenco guitar. This would be the *least* useful for Janine's report on the history of flamenco music and dance.
6	*b*	*Lives and legends of flamenco* implies that the source will mostly offer stories about people who are associated with the art of flamenco. *A biographical history* further confirms that it will deal with the life stories of flamenco artists.
7	*c*	If Janine searches under *SUBJECT: flamenco,* the computer will retrieve the titles of all sources in the library that are *about* flamenco, even if they don't contain the word "flamenco" in the title.
8		**Flamenco** (The "Results" display shows that *Flamenco* is a film, which is available at the library as a video recording.)
9		**Record 6** (The "Results" display states that the book was *translated by Sheila Smith.* This indicates that the book was originally written in a language other than English.)
10	*c*	It is common for *phone books* to contain maps showing area codes.
11	*a*	The website for the U.S. Copyright Office is, as the name implies, an official website of the U.S. Government. Therefore, its information about copyright laws would be reliable.
12	*b*	This topic focuses on one athlete winning an event and would be the *most specific* of all the choices.
13	*d*	The form asks for the *primary* reason for enrollment, and indicates to "circle *one.*" Deni should determine which of her two reasons is her *main* reason for enrolling and circle that option only.
14	*a*	There is no request for "date of birth" on the form.
15	*b*	On the line for "evening" number, Deni should indicate that her evening number is the same as her daytime number.
16		**Cash** The form states, *"NO CASH ACCEPTED."*
		READING: Words in Context, Level A
3	*a*	The word *vivid* means *lively and distinctive,* the opposite of *dull and vague.*
4	*d*	To *ascertain* something means to *determine* it.
5	*a*	In this context, *explicit* means *precise* or *specific,* a word that appears in the next sentence.
6	*c*	If your résumé is *effective,* it will get you a job interview, so it will have been *successful.*
7		**unusual**

Answer Key

Question	Answer	READING: Words in Context, Level A (cont.)
8		temporary
9		scarce
10		identical
11		occasional
		READING: Recall Information, Level A
3		safety
4		15–30 seconds
5		**1.** Connect the jumper cables following the instructions. **2.** Let car with good battery function for 15–30 seconds. **3.** Start stalled car. **4.** Remove clamps.
6	a	The passage states that a landlord "cannot abuse the right of access . . . or use this right to *harass (repeatedly disturb)* the tenant."
7	d	The first paragraph of the passage lists the *conditions under which a landlord may lawfully enter a unit;* the second paragraph focuses on *lawful procedures for entering;* the third paragraph advises *tenants what to do if their rights are violated.*
8		24 hours
9		emergencies and abandonment
		READING: Construct Meaning, Level A
3	c	The article mentions that capoeira was unlawful for many years, and then thought poorly of by the mainstream culture. Thanks to the efforts of *mestres* to promote capoeira, it is now a highly respected art form.
4		life-affirming qualities
5		martial art
6		playing
7	d	This story is mainly about Jane Addams' lifelong efforts to improve the lives of poor and exploited people.
8	b	The story states, "When economic depression hit in 1893, Addams saw that treating the effects of poverty was insufficient. Addressing its causes, she campaigned for laws. . . ."
9	c	To "flourish" means *to grow* or *to thrive.* The fact that Hull House expanded to include many more features makes Hull House comparable to a "flourishing tree."
10	d	From what the story states, you can conclude that the 1893 depression made poverty worse, so Addams needed to find a more complete solution to the problem.

Answer Key

Question	Answer	READING: Construct Meaning, Level A (cont.)
11	*a*	The story states, "Throughout her life, depending on the nation's political climate, Addams sometimes drew violent criticism. . . ." You can conclude that by the time Addams received many awards, people's attitudes had changed enough to accept many of her aims as desirable.
12	*d*	The statement mentions the *isolation of many of the immigrants,* which means that they kept *separate from the rest of society.*
13	*b*	Addams indicates that there were roses very near the woman's home, but that the woman was not in the habit of leaving the street where she lived.
14	*d*	Addams recounts how the Italian woman believed that no roses grew in America. Of course, roses *did* grow in America; it was just that the woman had not left her street enough to see them.
15		**public parks**
16		**limited**
17		**contented, peaceful, friendly**
18	*b*	This story is mainly about a fisherman's experience when he happens upon an unknown community of people living in harmony and abundance.
19	*b*	In this context, *imposing* means impressive or grand. Imposing houses and good fields are signs that the village is prosperous, or wealthy.
20	*a*	In real life, it would be impossible for any place like the village described in the story to be completely hidden from the rest of the world.
21	*b*	The villagers do not want their happy, peaceful village to become like the outside world.
22	*c*	The poet wants readers to know about his trip.
23	*b*	The poet describes the jagged edges of the mountain outline.
24	*d*	A literary magazine is the only choice of publications that would probably contain a poem.
25	*c*	The poet believes that there is a lot of interesting history to be discovered in this old city.
26	*d*	The poet is curious about learning more about the city.
27	*b*	The poet describes the trip and the scenery in great detail.
		READING: Evaluate/Extend Meaning, Level A
3	*d*	This is the only phrase that would make sense in this case. Rosa Parks' arrest prompted a bus boycott.
4	*d*	Although the demonstrators faced violence and jail, they refused to give up their nonviolent resistance.
5	*b*	Dr. King's words are meant to *inspire* the crusaders to continue their civil rights struggle.

Answer Key

Question	Answer	
6	c	The words Dr. King uses give the speech a *solemn,* or *serious, dignified* tone.
7	d	Language like "rolls down like waters" and "mighty stream" suggests that righteousness is a powerful force that has a momentum that is difficult to stop.
8	d	The third paragraph focuses mainly on the need for civil rights devotees to persist in their efforts until African Americans' civil rights are recognized everywhere.
9	c	Civil rights activists are clearly Dr. King's intended audience, and you can conclude from his words that he wants to urge them onward in their struggle, while discouraging them from resorting to hatred or violence.
10	b	The first two paragraphs focus on avoiding hateful feelings, unethical or violent acts, and racially divisive strategies in the struggle for freedom.
11	a	"We can never be satisfied *as long as a Negro in Mississippi cannot vote....*" is an example of concrete language because it refers directly to a real and *specific* goal, without any use of figurative language.
12		**opinion, fact, fact, opinion, opinion**
13	a	This story is written most like a drama.
14	a	The author describes the nasturtiums as *gifts of scarlet butterfly-shaped blooms.*
15	b	Although Mrs. Politti was dismayed that the boy had given her nasturtium seeds, she discovered the *peace in the daily ritual of watering and checking* the plants and the *gifts of scarlet butterfly-shaped blooms.*
16	d	Mrs. Politti "gazed out at the granite lawn, *installed after her husband's death,*" and recalls, "In those days, there had been birdsong, and the tremulous dance of butterflies."
17	c	The nasturtium grows and blossoms after Mrs. Politti cares for it each day.
18	d	Mrs. Politti will probably give as much care to the little boy as she does to the nasturtiums.
19		**chirped, birdsong, cooing**
20	b	Maria is reminding Charles that they should remember what James likes to eat as they plan the dinner.
21	a	The main idea has to do with planning the dinner.
22	d	Maria demonstrates a lot of knowledge of food and cooking.
23	a	They are enjoying planning the dinner together.
24	d	Maria knows a lot about identifying and cooking different kinds of produce.
25	c	James really likes her chicken pot pie and is coming to dinner.

Answer Key

| --- | --- | --- |
3	*b*	This sentence shows the correct use of the possessive pronoun *their.*
4	*d*	This sentence shows the correct use of the possessive pronoun *his.*
5	*b*	This sentence shows the correct antecedent agreement.
6	*c*	This sentence shows the correct antecedent agreement.
7		**it**
8		**his**
9	*d*	This sentence expresses a condition in the future. *Will have gone* is the correct response.
10	*c*	This sentence expresses a condition in the past. *Had remembered* is the correct response.
11		**found** (The verb *went* indicates this sentence is in the past. *Found* is the past tense of *find.*)
12		**will make** (The expression *next week* indicates this sentence needs a verb in the future tense.)
13		**taken** (The verb *has* indicates that a perfect tense is needed. *Taken* is the correct form of the verb.)
14		**have been painting** (This form of the verb gives the idea that an action began in the past but is still continuing in the present.)
15	*b*	The subject and the verb agree in number.
16	*b*	The subject and the verb agree in number.
17	*a*	This is a superlative sentence and *least* is the correct superlative word.
18	*c*	This is a comparative sentence that needs an adverb. *More inexpensively* is the correct answer.
19		**better** (This is a comparative sentence and *better* is the correct comparative form for the adjective *good.*)
20		**later** (This is a comparative sentence and *later* is the correct comparative form for the adjective *late.*)
21		**more safely** (This is a comparative sentence and *more safely* is the correct comparative form for the adverb *safely.*)
22		**longest** (This is a superlative sentence and *longest* is the correct superlative form for the adverb *long.*)
23		**worst** (This is a superlative sentence and *worst* is the correct superlative form for the adverb *bad.*)
24	*d*	This sentence shows a correct use of the adjective *clear.*
25	*c*	This sentence shows a correct use of the adjective *bad.*

Answer Key

LANGUAGE: Usage, Level A (cont.)

Question	Answer	
26	*a*	This sentence shows a correct use of the adverb *painstakingly.*
27	*c*	This sentence shows a correct use of the adjective *expensive.*
28		**taught** (This verb is used in the sense of "to provide knowledge of, or instruct in.")
29		**adapt** (This verb is used in the sense of "to accommodate, adjust.")
30		**precedes** (This verb is used in the sense of "to come or exist before in time or order.")
31	*d*	This sentence shows a correct use of negatives.
32	*b*	This sentence shows a correct use of negatives.
33	*a*	This sentence shows a correct use of negatives.
34	*c*	The words *throughout history* give the clue to the correct tense of the verb.
35	*c*	This is the correct use of negatives.
36	*d*	*Except* is the correct verb and is used in the correct tense.
37	*b*	This sentence needs a superlative and *rarest* is the correct superlative for *rare.*
38	*d*	This is the correct tense for this sentence.

LANGUAGE: Sentence Formation, Level A

Question	Answer	
3	*b*	This sentence best combines the original sentences while keeping the same idea.
4	*a*	This sentence best combines the original sentences while keeping the same idea.
5	*a*	This sentence best combines the original sentences while keeping the same idea.
6	*d*	This sentence best combines the original sentences while keeping the same idea.
7	*d*	This sentence best combines the original sentences while keeping the same idea.
8	*c*	This sentence best combines the original sentences while keeping the same idea.
9	*c*	This is a clear sentence with correct use of verbs.
10	*b*	This sentence is complete and expresses a clear idea.
11	*c*	This sentence is complete and expresses a clear idea.
12	*a*	This sentence is clear and has no unnecessary repetition.
13	*d*	This sentence is clear and has no unnecessary repetition.

LANGUAGE: Paragraph Development, Level A

Question	Answer	
3	*d*	This sentence fits perfectly in the sequence.
4	*c*	This sentence fits perfectly in the sequence.

Answer Key

Question	Answer	LANGUAGE: Paragraph Development, Level A (cont.)
5	*a*	This sentence shows the correct connective word for the blank provided.
6	*b*	This sentence shows the correct connective word for the blank provided.
7	*a*	These sentences best support, or develop, the topic sentence.
8	*d*	These sentences best support, or develop, the topic sentence.
9	*b*	This sentence is unrelated to the paragraph's main idea.
10	*c*	This sentence is unrelated to the paragraph's main idea.
		LANGUAGE: Capitalization, Level A
3	*c*	This is the right way of writing the title of a work.
4	*d*	This is the right way of writing the name of a place.
5		**Last week I was in North Miami Beach. I had a wonderful vacation!**
6		**Shakespeare not only wrote tragedies and historical novels, but also comedies like *Much Ado About Nothing.***
		LANGUAGE: Punctuation, Level A
3	*a*	This sentence shows the correct end mark.
4	*c*	*Well* is an introductory element and the comma is correctly placed.
5	*b*	The expression *many of whom were children* is an explanation and is correctly separated by commas.
6	*d*	*If any* is a parenthetical expression and it is correctly separated by commas.
7	*d*	The word *however* is correctly separated by commas.
8	*c*	This sentence shows the correct use of commas.
9		**Ben's bags are all packed; he'll be on his way to Toledo this morning.**
10		**Exercising regularly is good for one's health; nevertheless, few people exercise enough.**
11		**Unfortunately, I was in the elevator when the electricity went out.**
12		**The apartment is furnished with a stove, a refrigerator, a table, and two chairs.**
		LANGUAGE: Writing Conventions, Level A
3	*d*	This sentence shows the correct use of the apostrophe.
4	*a*	This sentence shows the correct punctuation and quotation marks.
5	*d*	This is the correct way of writing the date in a formal letter.
6	*b*	This is the correct way of writing an address.

Answer Key

Question	Answer	LANGUAGE: Writing Conventions, Level A (cont.)
7	*a*	This is the correct way of writing a salutation in a formal letter.
8	*a*	This is the correct way of writing a closing in a formal letter.
9		**May 30, 2006**
10		**112 Byron St.**
11		**Dear Mrs. Wong:**
12		**Technicians'** (This is a plural word. Insert the apostrophe after the first *s* and delete the final -*es*.)
13		**technicians?"** (The sentence quoted is a question, so the question mark should be inside the quotation marks.)
14		**Very truly yours,**
		SPELLING: Vowel, Level A
3		The misspelled word is *catigory*. The correct spelling is **category**.
4		The misspelled word is *idially*. The correct spelling is **ideally**.
5	*a*	The correct spelling is **conceive**.
6	*a*	The correct spelling is **ridiculous**.
7	*d*	The correct spelling is **endeavor**.
8	*b*	The correct spelling is **cumulative**.
9	*b*	The correct spelling is **ludicrous**.
10		The correct spelling is **maneuver**.
11		The correct spelling is **institute**.
12		The correct spelling is **veterinarian**.
13		The correct spelling is **fundamental**.
		SPELLING: Consonant, Level A
3	*d*	The correct spelling is **pungent**.
4	*c*	The correct spelling is **impetuous**.
5	*d*	The correct spelling is **committed**.
6		The correct spelling is **roughness**.
7		The correct spelling is **spacious**.
8		The correct spelling is **predecessor**.

Answer Key

Question	Answer	SPELLING: Consonant, Level A (cont.)
9		The misspelled word is *incesant.* The correct spelling is **incessant.**
10		The misspelled word is *stratejic.* The correct spelling is **strategic.**
		SPELLING: Structural Unit, Level A
3	*c*	The correct spelling is **distributors.**
4	*b*	The correct spelling is **consumer.**
5	*c*	*Sensor* and *censor* are homonyms, but **sensor** is the correct word choice for the sentence.
6	*d*	*Populace* and *populous* are homonyms, but **populace** is the correct word choice for the sentence.
7	*c*	The correct spelling is **recipient.**
8	*c*	The correct spelling is **impatience.**
9		The correct spelling is **capability.**
10		The correct spelling is **insistence.**
11		The misspelled word is *bridal.* The correct spelling is **bridle.**
12		The misspelled word is *existance.* The correct spelling is **existence.**

Building Skills with TABE®
Tests of Adult Basic Education

Student Answer Booklet

Level A: Reading, Language, Spelling

Name: _____   Date: _____

Organization/Program: _____

Directions: After you have talked with your teacher, circle the skill sections below that you need to work on. Turn to those skill sections in the workbook that match the skill sections circled below. Then find the same skill sections in this answer booklet. Fill in the correct bubble or write your answer on the lines provided. Answer the questions **only** for the sections that are circled. Please do not mark your answers in the workbook.

SKILL SECTIONS	WORKBOOK PAGE
READING	
Interpret Graphic Information	4
Words in Context	16
Recall Information	22
Construct Meaning	28
Evaluate/Extend Meaning	46
LANGUAGE	
Usage	62
Sentence Formation	80
Paragraph Development	90
Capitalization	98
Punctuation	104
Writing Conventions	110
SPELLING	
Vowel	118
Consonant	124
Structural Unit	128

READING   Interpret Graphic Information

1 ⓐ ⓑ ⓒ ⓓ   7 ⓐ ⓑ ⓒ ⓓ   13 ⓐ ⓑ ⓒ ⓓ

2 ⓐ ⓑ ⓒ ⓓ   8 _____   14 ⓐ ⓑ ⓒ ⓓ

3 ⓐ ⓑ ⓒ ⓓ   9 _____   15 ⓐ ⓑ ⓒ ⓓ

4 ⓐ ⓑ ⓒ ⓓ   10 ⓐ ⓑ ⓒ ⓓ   16 _____

5 ⓐ ⓑ ⓒ ⓓ   11 ⓐ ⓑ ⓒ ⓓ

6 ⓐ ⓑ ⓒ ⓓ   12 ⓐ ⓑ ⓒ ⓓ

READING   Words in Context

1 ⓐ ⓑ ⓒ ⓓ

2 ⓐ ⓑ ⓒ ⓓ

3 ⓐ ⓑ ⓒ ⓓ

4 ⓐ ⓑ ⓒ ⓓ

5 ⓐ ⓑ ⓒ ⓓ

6 ⓐ ⓑ ⓒ ⓓ

7	ordinary	*unusual*
8	permanent	
9	abundant	
10	diverse	
11	perpetual	

READING   Recall Information

1 ⓐ ⓑ ⓒ ⓓ

2 ⓐ ⓑ ⓒ ⓓ

3 _____

4 _____

5

	Connect the jumper cables following the instructions.
	Start stalled car.
	Remove clamps.
	Let car with good battery function for 15–30 seconds.

6 ⓐ ⓑ ⓒ ⓓ

7 ⓐ ⓑ ⓒ ⓓ

8 _____

9 _____

2

1. (a) (b) (c) (d)

2. (a) (b) (c) (d)

3. (a) (b) (c) (d)

4. _____ .

5. _____ .

6. _____

7. (a) (b) (c) (d)

8. (a) (b) (c) (d)

9. (a) (b) (c) (d)

10. (a) (b) (c) (d)

11. (a) (b) (c) (d)

12. (a) (b) (c) (d)

13. (a) (b) (c) (d)

14. (a) (b) (c) (d)

15. _____ .

16. _____ .

17. _____   _____   _____

18. (a) (b) (c) (d)

19. (a) (b) (c) (d)

20. (a) (b) (c) (d)

21. (a) (b) (c) (d)

22. (a) (b) (c) (d)

23. (a) (b) (c) (d)

24. (a) (b) (c) (d)

25. (a) (b) (c) (d)

26. (a) (b) (c) (d)

27. (a) (b) (c) (d)

1 ⓐ ⓑ ⓒ ⓓ

2 ⓐ ⓑ ⓒ ⓓ

3 ⓐ ⓑ ⓒ ⓓ

4 ⓐ ⓑ ⓒ ⓓ

5 ⓐ ⓑ ⓒ ⓓ

6 ⓐ ⓑ ⓒ ⓓ

7 ⓐ ⓑ ⓒ ⓓ

8 ⓐ ⓑ ⓒ ⓓ

9 ⓐ ⓑ ⓒ ⓓ

10 ⓐ ⓑ ⓒ ⓓ

11 ⓐ ⓑ ⓒ ⓓ

12

Dr. King's most moving speech was the prophetic "I've Been to the Mountaintop," delivered the day before his assassination.	*Opinion*
In 1964, at age 35, Dr. King was the youngest man in history to be awarded the Nobel Peace Prize.	
Dr. King was assassinated in Memphis, Tennessee, on April 4, 1968.	
Dr. King's death was the greatest national tragedy of the twentieth century.	
It is unfortunate that few remember King for his efforts on behalf of economic justice.	

13 ⓐ ⓑ ⓒ ⓓ

14 ⓐ ⓑ ⓒ ⓓ

15 ⓐ ⓑ ⓒ ⓓ

16 ⓐ ⓑ ⓒ ⓓ

17 ⓐ ⓑ ⓒ ⓓ

18 ⓐ ⓑ ⓒ ⓓ

19 1._____

2._____

3._____

20 ⓐ ⓑ ⓒ ⓓ

21 ⓐ ⓑ ⓒ ⓓ

22 ⓐ ⓑ ⓒ ⓓ

23 ⓐ ⓑ ⓒ ⓓ

24 ⓐ ⓑ ⓒ ⓓ

25 ⓐ ⓑ ⓒ ⓓ

LANGUAGE Usage

1 (a) (b) (c) (d)

2 (a) (b) (c) (d)

3 (a) (b) (c) (d)

4 (a) (b) (c) (d)

5 (a) (b) (c) (d)

6 (a) (b) (c) (d)

7 _____

8 _____

9 (a) (b) (c) (d)

10 (a) (b) (c) (d)

11 _____

12 _____

13 _____

14 _____

15 (a) (b) (c) (d)

16 (a) (b) (c) (d)

17 (a) (b) (c) (d)

18 (a) (b) (c) (d)

19 _____

20 _____

21 _____

22 _____

23 _____

24 (a) (b) (c) (d)

25 (a) (b) (c) (d)

26 (a) (b) (c) (d)

27 (a) (b) (c) (d)

28 _____

29 _____

30 _____

31 (a) (b) (c) (d)

32 (a) (b) (c) (d)

33 (a) (b) (c) (d)

34 (a) (b) (c) (d)

35 (a) (b) (c) (d)

36 (a) (b) (c) (d)

37 (a) (b) (c) (d)

38 (a) (b) (c) (d)

LANGUAGE Sentence Formation

1 (a) (b) (c) (d)

2 (a) (b) (c) (d)

3 (a) (b) (c) (d)

4 (a) (b) (c) (d)

5 (a) (b) (c) (d)

6 (a) (b) (c) (d)

7 (a) (b) (c) (d)

8 (a) (b) (c) (d)

9 (a) (b) (c) (d)

10 (a) (b) (c) (d)

11 (a) (b) (c) (d)

12 (a) (b) (c) (d)

13 (a) (b) (c) (d)

LANGUAGE   Paragraph Development

1 (a) (b) (c) (d)   6 (a) (b) (c) (d)

2 (a) (b) (c) (d)   7 (a) (b) (c) (d)

3 (a) (b) (c) (d)   8 (a) (b) (c) (d)

4 (a) (b) (c) (d)   9 (a) (b) (c) (d)

5 (a) (b) (c) (d)   10 (a) (b) (c) (d)

LANGUAGE   Capitalization

1 (a) (b) (c) (d)   5 _____

2 (a) (b) (c) (d)   6 _____

3 (a) (b) (c) (d)   _____

4 (a) (b) (c) (d)

LANGUAGE   Punctuation

1 (a) (b) (c) (d)   7 (a) (b) (c) (d)

2 (a) (b) (c) (d)   8 (a) (b) (c) (d)

3 (a) (b) (c) (d)   9 _____

4 (a) (b) (c) (d)   10 _____

5 (a) (b) (c) (d)   11 _____

6 (a) (b) (c) (d)   12 _____

LANGUAGE   Writing Conventions

1 (a) (b) (c) (d)   8 (a) (b) (c) (d)

2 (a) (b) (c) (d)   9 _____

3 (a) (b) (c) (d)   10 _____

4 (a) (b) (c) (d)   11 _____

5 (a) (b) (c) (d)   12 _____

6 (a) (b) (c) (d)   13 _____

7 (a) (b) (c) (d)   14 _____

6

SPELLING   Vowel

1 (a) (b) (c) (d)

2 (a) (b) (c) (d)

3 _____

4 _____

5 (a) (b) (c) (d)

6 (a) (b) (c) (d)

7 (a) (b) (c) (d)

8 (a) (b) (c) (d)

9 (a) (b) (c) (d)

10 _____

11 _____

12 _____

13 _____

SPELLING   Consonant

1 (a) (b) (c) (d)

2 (a) (b) (c) (d)

3 (a) (b) (c) (d)

4 (a) (b) (c) (d)

5 (a) (b) (c) (d)

6 _____

7 _____

8 _____

9 _____

10 _____

SPELLING   Structural Unit

1 (a) (b) (c) (d)

2 (a) (b) (c) (d)

3 (a) (b) (c) (d)

4 (a) (b) (c) (d)

5 (a) (b) (c) (d)

6 (a) (b) (c) (d)

7 (a) (b) (c) (d)

8 (a) (b) (c) (d)

9 _____

10 _____

11 _____

12 _____